WORK, SOCIETY, and CULTURE

WORK, SOCIETY, AND CULTURE

YVES R. SIMON

Edited by
Vukan Kuic

Fordham University Press
New York

Printed in the United States of America

Contents

Acknowledgments

THIS BOOK HAD ITS ORIGIN in the course on "Work and the Workman" given by Yves Simon at the University of Chicago in the spring quarter of 1958. The lectures were recorded on tape by Mr. Richard Marco Blow, and Simon made some corrections and added a few marginal remarks on the transcript. In 1965, William J. Sullivan produced a draft manuscript under the title "Work and the Working Man." All this material, with the addition of Simon's notes for the lectures delivered at Gonzaga University, Spokane, Washington, in the summer of 1959 and the notes from his file on "Work" from the Jacques Maritain Center at the University of Notre Dame, was made available to me in the fall of 1965.

In editing this book, I have followed essentially the same procedure that I used in editing Simon's *The Tradition of Natural Law* (1965): to reproduce both the spirit and the word of his lectures as faithfully as possible. The transition from the spoken to the written word, however, has required some adjustments both in the order and in the tone of the exposition, for which I assume the responsibility proper to an editor. I also decided on a new title. Some of the references were supplied in the transcript, while others had to be traced, and this led me to still other works which I thought worth including. For the sake of simplicity, however, I have decided to use only one kind of footnote.

My first debt of gratitude is to Mrs. Paule Yves Simon, not only for trusting me with another of her late husband's manuscripts,

vii

but also for helping me prepare it for publication. I am also grateful to Anthony O. Simon for supplying valuable bibliographical information about his father's work. The Research Committee of the College of Arts and Sciences at the University of South Carolina contributed to this project with a grant in the summer of 1967. I am grateful to Professor James E. Larson, Head of the Department of Political Science at the University of South Carolina, for his encouragement and support. Professor Dante Germino, of the University of Virginia, read an earlier version of the manuscript and made helpful comments. Miss Lynn Mahaffey of the University of South Carolina suggested a number of stylistic improvements in Chapter 1. Miss Julia Anne Moore helped to trace many of the references. Miss Stella Artemes, Mrs. Elaine C. Bright, and Miss Gloria C. Smith typed the manuscript. I acknowledge their services with gratitude. Last but not least, I wish to thank Mr. H. George Fletcher, Editor of Fordham University Press, for those finishing touches on the manuscript that make all the difference in reading the book.

In the Preface to *The Tradition of Natural Law*, I was not quite sure whether an editor is entitled to dedicate a book which after all is not his; nonetheless, I dedicated it to "other students of Yves R. Simon, past and future." Since then, I have come to the conclusion that such a dedication is not inappropriate, even as I realized that mine was redundant. Therefore, with Mrs. Simon's full concurrence, I should like to dedicate this book simply—

to the reader.

Editor's Preface

Yves René Simon was born in Cherbourg, France, on March 14, 1903. He came to the United States in 1938, and died in South Bend, Indiana, on May 11, 1961. He is one of the great thinkers and teachers of our time.

The purpose of this Preface is to give those readers who do not know Simon some indication of his mastery of philosophical subjects and his grasp of contemporary social problems, and to say a word that may be helpful in evaluating *Work, Society, and Culture.*

Simon studied several subjects, including natural science and medicine, but at the age of twenty-four he decided to dedicate his life to philosophy. With several degrees from the Sorbonne and the Catholic Institute of Paris, he taught philosophy at the Catholic University of Lille from 1930 to 1938, at the University of Notre Dame from 1938 to 1948, and at the University of Chicago from 1948 to 1959. He also lectured at many other institutions in France, Canada, Mexico, and the United States. And all during his working life, he wrote steadily, mostly on philosophical but on occasion also on political topics.

A bibliography of Simon's published work, compiled by his son Anthony O. Simon, constituted the Appendix to the first edition. It comprises over one hundred and thirty items, including books, articles, translations, and reviews, and collections edited by Simon. The sheer bulk of the published material, however, is only a very superficial sign of Simon's contribution to philosophy and to the understanding of contemporary experiences. One gets a much better perspective if one learns, for instance, that Simon's doctoral dissertation was on a subject that not many philosophers have dealt with before or after. *Introduction à l'ontologie du connaître* was first published in Paris in 1934; it was reprinted in the United States in 1965. It is still unique.

A moving testimony to the quality of Simon's work has been provided by Mortimer Adler and Peter Wolff in the recently published *Freedom of Choice* (1969). Wolff, who edited the English version of this book, was an Assistant Director of the Institute for Philosophical Research in San Francisco when that organization did a massive research on the problem of Freedom. Mortimer Adler wrote the two-volume study *The Idea of Freedom,* based on that research. Having read practically everything that has ever been written on the subject, they both concluded that Simon's *Freedom of Choice* stands out from the rest—at the very least among the works of contemporary philosophers. Dr. Adler, who met Simon not long after Simon came to the United States, writes:

This book . . . is the perfect antidote for the errors, the misunderstandings—or worse, the ignorances—that beset the modern discussion of free choice. Even a reader who comes to this book with little or no knowledge of the philosophical literature on the subjects that it treats cannot fail to appreciate its remarkable clarity, its felicitous combination of detailed concreteness with abstract precision, its exploration of common experience and its elucidation of common sense, and, above all, the intelligibility, reasonableness and fairness of its exposition of free choice not only in the context of opposing views but also in the context of all relevant psychological, ethical, and metaphysical considerations —the meaning of voluntariness and of responsibility, the role of the passions, the promptings of desire and the aspirations of love, the pursuit of happiness, the limitations of reason, the aspirations of the will, and the several principles of causality in their relation to one another and as they operate in the realms of matter and spirit or in the singularly human conjunction of body and mind [Foreword, pp. xi–xii].

The same can be said—and has been said, in different words —about every publication of Simon. Such high praise and virtually complete absence of unfavorable criticism is the result primarily of Simon's practice of writing and speaking strictly on what he knew something about—which means that he always knew exactly what he was speaking or writing about. He himself put it somewhat differently. Teaching, he used to say, is an overflow of contemplation. This definition, as his former students well know, applies especially to Simon's own teaching. It will not take too many pages for the new reader to get its meaning.

What Simon knew and had something worthwhile to say about is quite amazing. He had a plan for a complete "Philosophical Encyclopedia," and he probably would have completed most of it had he not died at the age of fifty-eight. Knowing the nature of his illness, he decided a few years before his death to change the title of the project to "Philosophical Inquiries," in which he was to take up only the key topics for a thorough examination, incorporating the rest of the subjects with somewhat less elaboration. The topics for which the material was collected more or less completely numbered twenty-one, but as Paule Simon has told us (*New Scholasticism* 32 No. 4), there was not enough time left to complete even this reduced plan. Nevertheless, from the papers he left behind there have already been produced by his former students and friends six books, including this one, and more are forthcoming. For the new readers, however, the range of Simon's philosophical interests and competence is perhaps best illustrated by the following list of different courses he taught in the Committee on Social Thought at the University of Chicago from 1948 to 1959:

Freedom of Choice and the Ethics of Liberty
The Object of Aristotelian Logic
General Metaphysics of Knowledge
Nature of Practical Wisdom
Causality and Contingency
Definition of Philosophy
Pre-Marxian Socialism
Non-Marxian Socialism: Proudhon
Introduction to Metaphysics
On Motion, Place, and Time
On Unity and Plurality in the Physical Universe
The Problem of Life
The Problem of Memory
From Experience to Understanding
Liberty and Community
Political Government
General Theory of Authority
The Theory of Being
The Metaphysics of Love
Theoretical Philosophy in Its Relation to the Sciences
Foundations of Ethics
Theory of Virtues
The Problem of Natural Law
On Work and the Workman
Nature and Forms of Analogy
The Critique of Scientific Knowledge

Everyone and especially the experts will agree that this is an impressive list for any teacher of philosophy. But Simon was not just a teacher of philosophic subjects. He was a true philosopher. He was always interested in existential political experience, and his comments on politics reveal the same insight and assurance found in his academic works. Simon's major political books are *La campagne d'Éthiopie et la pensée politique française, La grande crise de la République Française* (translated as *The Road to Vichy: 1918–1938), La marche à la délivrance* (translated as *The March to Liberation*), and *Par delà l'expérience du désespoir* (translated as *Community of the Free*). Though written mostly on the great issues of the Second World War, these books are more than just tracts for the times. They illuminate that great struggle in such a way that when re-read today they make us understand quite clearly why those enormous sacrifices have produced such limited achievements.

In the present context, however, Simon's grasp of political events and of forces at work in the world can best be illustrated by a statement he made to Edmond Michelet on June 12, 1940. Michelet, who is at this writing Minister for Cultural Affairs in the French Government, kept in close touch with Simon on political developments after Simon had left for the United States to accept the position of "visiting professor" at the University of Notre Dame. In the letter in question, Simon wrote: "The Nazis will not win this war; it will be won by the United States, but God only knows at what price in suffering for our country." Today this reads as a statement of fact. But as Michelet points out, the statement was made six days before the famous appeal by Charles DeGaulle to the French to continue fighting and eighteen months before the attack on Pearl Harbor and the consequent American entry into the war. Not many Frenchmen, or many Americans for that matter, either in America or in France, saw it quite that way at that time.

To have developed such an insight into matters political—
which really are unpredictable—while at the same time acquiring such a sure grasp of so many of the hardest philosophical problems, Simon clearly had to be a special kind of
man. He was. He was humble and strong, and he possessed
these qualities to such a degree that anyone who ever met him
immediately sensed the presence of a great man. On his job,
as Leo Ward has recorded, he used the simplest means: a
desk, a few books, some notebooks, paper and pencil—and
hard work (*Commonweal* 74 No. 14). But he boldly attacked
problems which had caused difficulties to the greatest minds
in the history of philosophy. "Courage," he once said, "is a
thing which a philosopher needs an excess of for many reasons,
the first of which is the weight of past failure." Another reason for which a philosopher needed courage, according to
Simon, was that when he discovered a truth it was his duty
to express it with conviction and zeal, leading inescapably to
the implication that he, the solitary fighter, knew better about
the really important issues than some of the greatest minds
among the philosophical geniuses. On this subject, too, Simon
knew what he was talking about:

It looks as though a painter of fair talent went to war against
Leonardo da Vinci, Michelangelo, and Rubens. How can the
philosopher convince people that he is not just yielding to insane
pride? The audacity with which he discusses, criticizes, and re-
futes genius bears all the appearances of the worst kind of conceit.
Can anything be done to remove these damaging appearances?
Much can be done, indeed; but to conceal certainty by proposing
truth under the externals of socially acceptable opinion is not always the right method. The job has to be done through things that
are much more difficult to acquire than good social manners. These
things are virtues, and accordingly they are hard to get. In the fulfillment of the philosopher's duty there is no substitute for the

fearless love of truth, for selflessness, fortitude, and humility ["The Philosopher's Calling," 1958].

The reader will have no difficulty recognizing this kind of approach in the pages that follow. In them there is no understatement of truth as Simon saw it, but this truth is offered with utter selflessness.

Work was one of those hard philosophical topics which had interested Simon since his student days. He published his first article on the subject in 1936, and two years later he elaborated his thoughts in a monograph entitled *Trois leçons sur le travail*. Parts of these lectures were translated and published in English in 1940. By 1947, Simon had further refined his views, and he presented his new position under the title "The Concept of Work," as a contribution to a symposium called *The Works of the Mind*. Thus by the time he offered a course on "Work and the Workman" at the University of Chicago in 1958, he was offering the results of more than twenty years of progressive study and reflection on the subject, considered not as a narrow specialty but in the context of related and equally profound philosophical topics.

In the conclusion to "The Problem of Natural Law," which was the course he gave just before the one on "Work and the Workman," Simon suggested that what has commonly been called "social justice" in modern times admits of interpretation in terms of natural law. But he also warned that the subject should be approached with extremely flexible and subtle instruments. In his next course, he supplied these instruments.

While the reader will judge for himself, this book in my opinion contains nothing less than a complete prescription, difficult to fill but realistic, on how it may be possible to save the modern man from himself. To put it very simply, what Simon calls for is the reintegration of both work *and* culture into society through the development of a culture based not on leisure but on work-like activities. We are all aware that one of the most persistent modern themes is that of alienation, reputed to affect particularly those who actually contribute most to society's survival, the providers of the so-called nobler things in life not excluded. Workers, artists, and intellectuals—but not necessarily for the same reasons—often feel that they do not belong in modern society. That is a fact of modern experience. But really to find out why they feel that way, one must have some idea of the place of work, art, and intellect in society, which in turn is ultimately impossible without an understanding of the nature not only of society and of justice but also of work, art, and the intellect itself. Simon knows all these subjects well, and he knows how to expound them. But above all, he sees and presents them in their deepest interconnectedness which is only rarely even approached by other writers on contemporary social experience. For many readers, Simon's exposition is bound to come as a revelation. I have acknowledged my enlightment in the choice of the title for the book.

VUKAN KUIC

University of South Carolina
Columbia
June, 1970

1

The Concept of Work

THE DAILY LIFE OF MAN is composed of things whose meaning is hidden in the mystery of their familiarity. Work is one of these. Other examples would be love, companionship, sincerity, honor, sport, ennui, and community-feeling. Many would think that those things need not be defined; but let us be aware that the feeling of familiarity we experience when we speak of honor or of work is not caused by the kind of intelligibility which places an object above definition. St. Augustine says of time that he knows what it is if no one asks him, but no longer knows if he has to explain it.[1] Time needs to be defined. Its familiarity is not that of a primary notion, and

[1] "*Si nemo ex me quaeret, scio; si quaerenti explicare velim, nescio*" (*Confessionum* Liber XI, Cap. XIV). The passage in the translation by Edward B. Pusey reads: "What then is time? If no one asks me, I know; if I wish to explain to one that asketh, I know not; yet I say boldly that I know, that if nothing passed away, time past were not; and if nothing were coming, a time to come were not; and if nothing were, time present were not" (*The Confessions of Saint Augustine* [New York: Modern Library, 1949], p. 253).

1

"work" is immensely farther than "time" from the condition of primary intelligibility.

Being anterior to any definition, however, is only one of two causes of indefinability; the other is the lack of essential unity. A complex whose components are not comprised within one essence cannot be defined. For instance, it is possible to define the physician, and it is possible to define the singer; but it is not possible to define the singer who is also a physician, or the physician who is also a singer. Thus our second problem is that right now we cannot be sure whether the term "worker" conveys an essence or a mere aggregate of intelligibilities. Indeed, as Werner Sombart would have it, the word might be without any real meaning, albeit usable in conversation because meanings may be assigned to it at will.[2] And so all that can be said at this point, even assuming work to be an essence, is that determining the approach from which the intelligible unity of work may be perceived remains a difficult problem.

Progress toward a definition of work is hampered also by an entirely extrinsic factor. It is customary to set in opposition workers and idlers, and no one wants to be an idler. In daily language there is a sharp contrast between the worker and the fellow who, because he does not work, is considered to be a parasite; consequently, everyone wants to be a worker. Now, people probably have disliked being considered lazy and good-for-nothing at all times; but modern society actually exalts work, which is in sharp contrast with the attitudes prevalent in classical cultures. For instance, in the chapter on Pericles, Plutarch remarks that no well-born young man would want to be Phidias. A gentleman enjoys the contemplation of the

[2] " 'Arbeiter' ist eines jener völlig sinnlosen Worte, mit denen wir unsere geselligen, politischen und wissenschaftlichen Unterhaltungen zu bestreiten pflegen. Das jeder sich etwas anderes dabei denken kann, macht es für diese besonders geeignet" (*Handwörterbuch der Staatswissenschaften* [Jena: Fischer, 1909]).

sculptor's masterpieces, but he would never himself use hammer and chisel and get covered with sweat and dust.[3] The story of the life and death of Michelangelo seems to indicate that similar attitudes toward art and work prevailed also in the Renaissance. Even as late as 1789, Edmund Burke wrote that the occupation of a hairdresser or of a candlemaker could not be a matter of honor to any person—"to say nothing of a number of other more servile employments." [4] But during the nineteenth century, in the years following the fall of Napoleon when war-weary people turned to industry, there developed a new society in which it became honorable to be called a hard, obstinate, and indefatigable worker. For several generations, the main beneficiary of this new outlook was the so-called captain of industry. Quite often, this was a man who, though he might have worked with his hands when he was young, now had too much money to be a menial worker; nevertheless he kept driving himself and other people practically to death. More recently, the class of men who actually work with their hands, the working class, has obtained much of that social consideration for which it had often fought with such intense bitterness, and in most countries workers are incessantly extolled in the rhetoric of all political parties. Thus, considering that no one wants to be an idler, and considering, further, that for over a century workers have been gaining in social prestige, we must realize that any search for a definition of work today will be exposed to the pressure of

[3] *Plutarch's Lives* (New York: Modern Library, 1932), p. 183.

[4] The passage continues: "Such descriptions of men ought not to suffer oppression from the state; but the state suffers oppression if such as they, either individually or collectively, are permitted to rule." Burke denies that his view is based on prejudice, and in a footnote he quotes Ecclesiasticus 38: 24, 25, 27, 33, 34. The first two verses read: "The wisdom of a learned man cometh by opportunity of leisure; and he that hath little business shall become wise"; "How can he get wisdom that holdeth the plow, and that glorieth in the goad; that driveth oxen; and is occupied in their labors; and whose talk is of bullocks?" *Reflections on the Revolution in France*, ed. Thomas H. D. Mahoney (New York: Liberal Arts Press, 1955), p. 56.

a successful ideology. This is precisely the kind of pressure that a philosopher must be ready to resist.

In 1936, I published a definition of work by which I and most of my readers were either excluded from the respected genus of workers or were, at best, relegated into groups of people who could be called workers only in a qualified sense.[5] Insofar as my paper attracted any attention, I had practically everyone against me. I tried in vain to make my critics understand that their anger was comic. I had taken all possible precautions to show that in order to be good-for-something, and to be good absolutely, it was not indispensable to be a worker. I had never postulated that work was the only honorable way of spending one's energy; there was no reason, therefore, for any of my readers to be offended. But some were, and I learned something from that minor incident. In that first endeavor to define work, I had let the sociological perspective which drastically narrows the concept somehow appear decisive. Here, I propose to analyze work from the metaphysical, psychological, and ethical points of view in addition to the sociological, and fewer persons should feel left out of the general category. Those who still may not qualify as workers will have good reasons not to mind it.

Good method requires that the search for a definition should start with the most unmistakable case. Accordingly, we shall first consider the case of the manual workers, rather than that of the lawyer, merchant, or scholar. We all agree that there is no context in which, say, carpenters or masons would be set in opposition to workers; but we can readily think of several contexts in which no one would hesitate to set in opposition worker and scholar, worker and merchant, worker and lawyer. Again, this is merely a question of order,

---

[5] "La Définition du travail," *Revue de Philosophie* (Paris), N.S., 6 (1936), 426–441. See also Yves R. Simon, *Trois leçons sur le travail* (Paris: Téqui, 1938).

and priority does not imply exclusion. We do not say that lawyers or physicists are not and should never be called workers; but by considering masons and carpenters—that is, manual workers—in the first place, we are sure to start our analysis with cases in which the thing to be analyzed is most certainly present.

MANUAL WORK

In both theory and popular usage, manual work is distinguished from any other kind of work by its direct relation to physical nature. What the word "direct" excludes here is the human intermediary; the tools and the machines are by no means excluded. For instance, to till the land with a tractor-driven plow is manual work; but the gentleman farmer who merely gives orders to his farm hands is not a manual worker even though he may be a worker in some sense.

The other characteristic features of manual work, which may be less familiar but are no less self-evident, are the following:

1. Manual work is a transitive activity. While this term also means transient, fluid, nonlasting, "transitive" here designates the property of passing from an agent into a receiver. Also, in some metaphysical contexts a transitive action is defined simply as the production of an effect, and thus an action whose effect remains within the agent is still considered transitive. Here, transitive activity is understood in a restricted sense to designate only those actions whose effect is external to the agent. Hammering, shaping, melting, cutting are transitive actions in this restricted and strongest sense. The agent whom we call a worker is acting upon an external matter: by his activity, a piece of hot iron is being beaten into shape, a board is being sawed, or bricks are being laid in a certain order.

Of course, there is always an effect left in the worker himself. But when this—rather than the effect on the external matter —becomes the specifying principle of activity, work is displaced by something else which we call play, sport, exercise, or indeed "make-work."

Movements which might be the acts of workers often are repeated by people at play, or by people who want to lose weight, or by people who want to discipline their passions. For instance, some ascetics make legs for chairs that will never be. What is their activity to be called? There is in it a kind of absurdity which may be accepted as a sacrifice, as an act of self-denial. Their activity may also satisfy a need for distraction within the requirements of a highly spiritual calling. We may call it asceticism, or we may call it play, but we cannot call it work except in a manner of speaking. A significant contrary example is the case of unemployed men paid for doing things known to be completely needless and useless. They understand that they are just being kept busy, that they are only apparently treated as workers and are actually considered idlers in need of paternal protection against the dangers of idling. In such a situation, we also detect, over and above the effects upon external nature, certain conditions conducive to social disturbance.

2. Manual work is an activity by way of change. It belongs to the physical type, in sharp opposition to the psychological operations which do, or at least may, exist by way of rest. To work is to bring about a change in an external matter. When that change has come to an end, the worker's activity belongs to the past. Like many metaphysical simplicities, this has far-reaching implications. To make a chair is to bring about a change in the wood, the nails, the straw, and the glue of which the chair is made. If that change has come to its ends—in other words, if the chair is finished—what can the carpenter do? He

may sit on the new chair and rest, he may sit in front of it and admire his work, he may go away and forget about carpentry, he may start making another chair, or he may destroy the chair that he has just made, if he is dissatisfied with it. The thing that he cannot do is to keep making a particular chair after this chair has been made.

Reasoning also is an activity by way of motion. In Hamlet's words, it is "the discourse of reason." Discoursing means running (*currere, discurrere*) from one object to another, from an antecedent to a conclusion. And when such a goal is attained, reasoning must come to an end. It is like climbing a hill. When I reach the top of a hill, I may contemplate the landscape, but I cannot continue to climb that hill. In intellectual life, reasoning and all forms of research are activities by way of change, which cannot go on when the term of change has been reached. Yet some psychological activities exist by way of rest. Contemplation is a kind of rest, and so is joy, whereas love admits of both ways. There is such a thing as love in desire, in struggle, in restless tendency, and there is such a thing as love in presence and joy. By love I can be moved to walk many miles to see a beloved person, but when at long last the beloved is present, love does not die out. The higher, the more perfect, the more genuine form of love exists, like contemplation and joy, in presence and by way of rest.

3. All the foregoing implies that manual work is a useful, not a terminal, activity. But notice that "useful" is often equated with "good," as if anything not useful could not be good in any way. Such language, which is bad in daily life, may be dreadfully deceptive in philosophy. A thing useful is that which leads to a desirable state of affairs; whatever is useful is relative to an excellence that lies beyond utility. However, the essentially useful character of an activity is often hidden by concomitant pleasure; and so in order to obtain a precise

notion of the useful and to see that it is not identical with
the good, we must think of operations that have no desirabil-
ity of their own and would not be desired at all if they did not
lead to objects of desire. Walking a few blocks from home to
school is a thing useful, but it is also pleasurable. An example
of a thing purely useful would be to walk the same distance
in a blizzard.

Work so definitely has the character of a useful activity
that, if the end is placed in the activity itself, what would be
work under other circumstances becomes something other
than work. For instance, it is very handy for a family to have
a man whose hobby is fixing and improving everything in the
house. Is this man working? The case is somewhat uncertain.
If he is doing things useful because they are needed, his activity is a sort of work. But if, having retired prematurely with
such means that he can hire all the help he pleases, he does
things by himself in order to avoid boredom, his activity is
really a hobby. The purpose being in the activity itself, it cannot be called work without qualification.

4. The proposition that manual, physical work is a rationally
directed activity sounds plausible enough, yet it raises interesting difficulties. A dam can be built according to the plans and
computations of an engineer, but long before engineers existed
beavers already knew how to build dams. Unless we most arbitrarily attribute reason to beavers we must admit that a dam
can be built in nonrational fashion, by instinct and animal
intelligence. Should we, then, say that building a dam is work
when it is directed by reason but is not work when direction
is supplied by nonrational powers? The relevance of this question does not concern beavers alone. Indeed, it is proper to
ask whether animals work, and whether work is a form of
activity common to man and brute. But something even more
important is at stake here. Within the human world, similar

results may be obtained sometimes empirically and sometimes in highly rational ways, and what we want to know is whether the notion of work is realized more genuinely in the case of the worker who understands and rationally directs his own action upon physical things or in that of the man whose skill is strictly empirical and is directed by mere habit.

We are all familiar with cases, occurring even in modern industry, in which a man of much experience and little learning may be more successful in a particular operation or process than a freshly trained engineer. Rational direction of work, however, is by no means excluded in such a comparison, as both these men know in some sense what they are doing. Indeed, examples of sheer "empirical skill" are not easy to find. But I have one from an eighteenth-century book relating a journey to Chile. There it is claimed that the best liquor is made by old Chilean women who chew corn and spit it into a sort of barrel. A little acquaintance with the formulas of starch, maltose, and alcohol, and with the action of amylase in the transformation of starch into maltose, makes it easy for us to understand that this may indeed be a good way of making corn liquor. We are even willing to believe that the drink made according to this old Chilean recipe might taste at least as good as the product of a modern scientific distillery. Yet the old women knew no chemistry; they just did, in their turn, what was done by their grandmothers. How it ever started we do not know, but we can safely assume that the method was discovered by luck rather than by rational inference. We also agree that these chewing and spitting women of Chile were working. But how shall we compare them with, say, highly skilled workers of modern industry, some of whom know a good deal of chemistry and use it in their work?

The fact is that the relation of manual work to its rules admits of two significantly different forms. The operations through which a man acts directly upon physical nature may be regulated by his own reason; but it also happens that the rules of such an operation remain unknown to the worker, except insofar as they are present in his habits. The two cases have to be expressed in concepts, and we are wondering which one of the two deserves more properly to be called work. For the present, we may avoid the problem by resorting to a simple distinction between unskilled and skilled labor. But what we really want to find out is whether rationality—i.e., rational direction of activity—should be included in a general, theoretical definition of work. How can we do that? I believe that it would be best to take a closer look at the works of the mind.

THE WORKS OF THE MIND

Let us begin by distinguishing among directions of rational processes. I use this vague expression deliberately, but I have a number of concrete examples in mind. For instance, an architect is the traditional symbol of man engaged in the rational process preparatory to manual work. Similarly, a scientist doing pure research is in the rational process preparatory to what we shall call contemplation. And finally, a statesman at work is engaged in the rational process that aims at bringing order into human society. These three directions of rational processes represent three distinct works of the mind which we want to consider more closely.[6]

What do architects or engineers do? They plan and direct manual work. That means that by their special knowledge they control physical activities which result in a building, a canal, or a machine. They are thus involved in an intellectual relation which because of its direction may be called, for short,

---

[6] See Yves R. Simon, "The Concept of Work," in *The Works of the Mind,* ed. R. B. Heywood (Chicago: University of Chicago Press, 1947), pp. 3–17.

"Man and Nature." I should like to retain this expression, if we can free it from a fundamental ambiguity which it has long harbored.

Ever since the time of the Renaissance, there has been a tendency to identify science with the rational process aimed at the shaping of nature according to man's purposes. We find this inclination in Leonardo da Vinci, in Francis Bacon, and in Descartes who proposed a science that would make men *"les maîtres et possesseurs de la nature."* [7] By the time of the Industrial Revolution in the nineteenth century, this reductionist view of science had become so prevalent that it finally caused a reaction. Among those who rejected the view that the only science was the science of nature was Auguste Comte. He believed that he had discovered a science for the control and transformation of society, which was superior to the science of nature.[8] But neither he nor any later positivist ever revised the opinion received from the Renaissance that scientific knowledge is strictly useful knowledge—that is, that science is desirable only for its demiurgical powers.[9] If we are to keep the expression "Man and Nature" to designate a certain relationship maintained by the mind, let us call it *technical knowledge* rather than science. Science is something else.

Speaking in general, scientific knowledge is useful to man

[7] See André Lalande, *Les théories de l'induction et de l'expérimentation* (Paris: Boivin, 1929), pp. 43–44.

[8] "The Positive spirit, so long confined to the simpler inorganic phenomena, has now passed through its difficult course of probation. It extends to a more important and more intricate class of speculations, and disengages them for ever from all theological or metaphysical influence. . . . A firm objective basis is consequently laid down for that complete coordination of human existence towards which all sound Philosophy had ever tended, but which the want of adequate materials has hitherto made impossible" (*A General View of Positivism*, trans. J. H. Bridges [London: Trübner, 1865], p. 37).

[9] "Quel est l'objet essentiel de la science? C'est d'accroître notre influence sur les choses"—Henri Bergson, *Évolution créatrice* (Paris: Alcan, 1909), p. 356.

in his social life as well as in his relation to nature, and the possession of this knowledge is usually quite rewarding to the scientist, personally. But science, strictly speaking, must also be seen as aiming toward the final purpose of discursive rational process as such, which we shall call contemplation of truth, or simply contemplation. In this discussion of work and of the works of the mind, it is very important to understand that contemplation itself is not work in any sense whatsoever.

To begin with, let us recall the most obvious characteristics of manual work: it is a transitive, external activity. By contrast, nothing is more obviously immanent than contemplation. Moreover, work is an activity by way of change; but one distinction of contemplation is precisely that it is of itself a motionless activity and a participation in eternal life. Surely, we cannot approach the meaning of eternity by trying to imagine a line with no end in the past and no end in the future. Rather, we begin to understand eternity by considering motionless activity such as happens when, after having spent a few days, or years, or a lifetime looking for a certain truth, at long last we have the result. I do not mean that this result can ever be so exhaustive as to exclude further research. No human apprehension is exclusive of further research; on the contrary, it always invites further research. But concerning some tiny particle of truth, we sometimes happen to have the right answer, and then we can stop, look, and listen. We are not inactive, yet our activity is not by way of change; it is motionless, it is eternity.[10] Unfortunately, in man, activity by way of rest is restricted and conditioned in a hundred ways. After five minutes, the contemplative has to move to shut the window, to take a glass of water, or to answer a call; or he must move simply because not moving causes a stultifica-

[10] See Yves R. Simon, *Introduction à l'ontologie du connaître* (Paris: Desclée de Brouwer, 1934; Dubuque, Iowa: Brown Reprint Library, 1965); "Activité immobile," pp. 104–107.

tion of imagination which makes further thought impossible. There is no need to minimize the hundred ways in which our contemplative activity is restricted; what is interesting and important is to grasp the nature of that activity within its restrictions.

Finally, contemplation stands in opposition to work in regard to the distinction between means and ends. Work is always useful, forever a means to some end. Contemplation, on the contrary, is always an end in itself and can thus never be useful. In fact, it is better than useful. People usually feel insulted when they are told that they are doing something which is not useful. Yet there are two ways in which something may be useless: its uselessness may be on this side of utility, and so a waste of time and effort; or it may be on the other side of utility, beyond utility. The latter is the case of contemplation, which is worthy of itself and by itself, independently of any further relation.

All this of course does not mean that the contents of scientific and technical knowledge and the contents of pure contemplation are contradictory. Even the popular newspapers recognize on occasion that many great technical discoveries were actually made by men who were not intent on the transformation of physical nature, but were engaged simply in the pursuit of truth. Moreover, truly great scientists seldom miss a chance to explain that if our schools were to let all scientific effort be completely polarized by technical purposes, technology would be the first to suffer.[11] Thus, even from a

---

[11] For instance, A. N. Whitehead writes: "The really profound changes in human life all have their ultimate origin in knowledge pursued for its own sake. The use of the compass was not introduced into Europe till the end of the twelfth century A.D., more than 3,000 years after its first use in China. The importance which the science of electromagnetism has since assumed in every department of human life is not due to the superior practical bias of Europeans, but to the fact that in the West electrical and magnetic phenomena were studied by men who were dominated by abstract theoretic interest" (*Introduction to Mathematics* [New York: Holt, 1911], pp. 32–33).

utilitarian social standpoint, it is indispensable that there be at least a few men interested not in technology but exclusively in what some have called the "honor of the human spirit." [12] We may call it, with greater propriety, the contemplation of truth. This intellectual interest, pointing in a direction distinct from that which relates man to physical nature, is what we call *science*. And the relation science strives to establish may then be called, for short, "Man and Truth."

But there are also rational processes which are aimed neither at the transformation of physical nature nor at the contemplation of truth. They are aimed at bringing about an order of wisdom in man, individual and social. The relation here involved may be called, for short, "Man and Mankind," and people are once again gradually realizing that a rational ordering of this relation is at least as important as control over nature. The trouble is, of course, that it is also much harder. We all know that good and appropriate ways of behaving toward ourselves, toward other persons, and in society are not innate to man. Such behavior is the result first of upbringing, and then, if this has been successful, of self-government. But this is a task which is never finished. When we think that it is almost accomplished, we discover that it has to be done all over again. For example, a man may be very temperate until the age of fifty and feel that he is immune from the temptations of intemperance. Then something happens, and the habits of temperance that seemed so steady—after so many years one would believe them to be unshakable—are broken and have to be repaired and rebuilt. The same situation holds for society at large. Even the best of constitutions or the most scientific organization of economic relations cannot guarantee smooth operation of the social order in perpetuity. We must

[12] The expression is attributed to Jacobi in Florian Cajori, *History of Mathematics*, 2nd edition (New York: Macmillan, 1919), p. 413.

all continuously work hard at it, so to speak, and public officials the hardest.

Among the rational processes whose purpose is to bring about and maintain social order, we may distinguish between those which are principal and those which are instrumental in character. By principal, I mean the functions of government itself, whether they be exercised in a small community like the township, in a state, or in a federation of states. What is directly intended by government at all levels is the establishment of order in the uses of human freedom.[13] Under every government, however, there are varieties of instrumental personnel, such as economists, administrators, military men, and policemen. It is of some importance to understand that rational processes are involved in these numerous tasks as well as in the principal task of government itself. For instance, while soldiers may not often think of themselves in these terms, a military force is in fact a rational instrument of social order. Unfortunately, it sometimes happens that the instrumental is so strong as to cripple the principal. One should not try to fix a watch with heavy tools. Likewise, if too much power is yielded to military men, all sorts of trouble may arise because of an essentially absurd situation in which men whose function is instrumental by essence are expected to act as leaders. This is sometimes the only alternative to anarchy, but it is never desirable except as such an alternative. The old rule that the military is to take orders from men whom we call either statesmen or politicians expresses an essential and everlasting social necessity. And the same rule applies in regard to all other instrumental personnel.

According to their directions, we have, then, this tripartite division of rational processes: man and nature, man and man-

[13] See Yves R. Simon, *A General Theory of Authority* (Notre Dame, Ind.: University of Notre Dame Press, 1962).

kind, and man and truth. Now if we abstract from social clas-
sifications and consider only the theoretical definition of work
derived from an analysis of *manual work*, there is nothing in
the concept of "work" that absolutely prevents it from being
applied to the activities of the architect or the engineer. What
these people do in fact is employ their minds in useful action
upon physical nature, albeit indirectly through human inter-
mediaries. We shall call such activities *technical work*. Similarly, there is nothing in rational action involving human beings that contradicts the overall theoretical definition of work.
True, such action is very different from manual and technical
work. People not only should not be but cannot be acted upon
like, say, rocks, timber, or steel at a building site. There is an
everlasting difference between human activities in regard to
things to be made and in regard to what is to be done with
people. A "social engineer" is a contradiction in terms and a
chimera.[14] But that does not mean that statesmen, administrators, or soldiers doing their job cannot be said to be working. They are doing what we shall call *social work*. Finally,
considering the activities of research scientists, we find that
they too reveal certain characteristic features of working activity, most notably those of change and utility. Clearly, research is a useful activity by way of motion, and there is really
no reason why it should not be called work. We may call it
research work or we may call it pure *intellectual work*. But let
us always remember that this third kind of the works of the
mind is ultimately directed toward contemplation, which is
not work in any sense whatsoever.

Notice now how nicely this way of interpreting the notion
of work in terms of change and utility agrees with common
opinion and daily language. We speak of manual workers as
real workers. Next come the engineers and other technical

[14] See Yves R. Simon, "From the Science of Nature to the Science of
Society," *The New Scholasticism*, 27, No. 3 (July 1953), 280–304.

workers of all kinds. Third in place are those whom we call social workers, that is, most civil servants as well as politicians, psychiatrists, teachers, priests, and so on. The fourth and last place on this sliding scale of activities arranged according to their closeness to manual work is reserved for the intellectual workers, such as mathematical physicists and other pure researchers. Notice also that, in principle, there is here no room for those who do nothing but contemplate. Yet, since usually a great deal of hard work is required before anyone is able to stop, look, and listen to the truth, not even professors of philosophy need be absolutely excluded from the general category of workers.

I believe that this brief account of the works of the mind has helped us to clarify the question whether manual work deserves the more accurately to be called "work" when it is directed by habit or when it is directed by reason. The least that can be said is that rationally directed operations, including manual labor, constitute a distinct species of activity and that there is nothing arbitrary about calling this species "work." Yet the fact remains that work predicated of social and intellectual activities is of recent usage, and that everything connected with science, morality, statecraft, and philosophy had traditionally been set in contrast to work. Because of this contrast, persons in daily and habitual contact with physical nature were not considered particularly rational, and were therefore never allowed to participate fully in public affairs. It is only in modern times that all these things have changed so radically. Does that mean, then, that Sombart was right after all, and that "worker" is now a word for strictly historical and partisan use? I do not think so. I think that it is possible to establish an objective concept of work, although it is clear that "work" cannot be defined in metaphysical terms alone and that the social component in its definition will in some sense be decisive. But before we consider the notion of work from the social standpoint, we must examine still another feature of manual work, and perhaps of all work, from the metaphysical point of view.

IRKSOMENESS OF WORK

In most European languages, the words for the Latin and English *labor* mean also extreme effort associated with pain. The Greek πόνος, the French *travail*, the German *Arbeit* are also used for the pangs of birth. According to Hannah Arendt, *labor* has the same etymological root as *labare* ("to stumble under a burden"); πόνος and *Arbeit* have the same etymological root as "poverty" (πενία in Greek, *Armut* in German). In medieval German, the word *Arbeit* is used to translate *labor, tribulatio, persecutio, adversitas, malum.*[15] Similarly, the French *travailler* is derived from *tripalium*, which was some kind of torture. These etymologies leave little doubt about the historical association of work with pain or irksomeness. This association seems to persist despite the changing attitudes toward work, and, indeed, the changing conditions of labor.

Here is a true story. One day I went fishing on the Gulf of Mexico with a young student friend who was telling me about his plans, and it seemed to me that they were not animated by any particular zeal for an industrious life. So with the kind of naïveté that can always be expected from a philosopher, I asked him whether he liked to work ten hours a day. He hesitated a moment and then said "No." Five minutes later, he returned to the subject by remarking that he did not quite understand my question. "How could I like to work ten hours a day?" he said. "If you asked me 'Do you like to play ten hours a day?' I would say 'Yes.' " Apparently the notion of strenuous effort was so closely associated in his mind with that of work

[15] *The Human Condition* (Chicago: University of Chicago Press, 1958), pp. 48n, 80n, 110n.

that my question meant to him, "Do you like to do something unpleasant ten hours a day?"

Obviously, there must be a reason for this consistent and close association of the idea of work and the idea of strenuous effort, pain, and irksomeness. But before we try to discover what that reason is, let us dare ask whether the connection holds purely and simply. In other words, is an activity considered work only if it is painful in some respect? It is granted that work is often, even commonly, difficult and painful; the testimony of experience is plain and unmistakable. If I do not like to play chess, I will not play chess. Most people who play chess do so because they like it, and they quit when they no longer like it. With work it is another story, for though most men and women work, quite a few never like it, and those who like it on the whole always dislike it once in a while, generally during a part of every day. That much is agreed. But does an activity cease to be work when it ceases to be painful?

To get an answer to this question, I should like first to compare work and virtue, without implying in any way that work is of itself a virtuous activity. The only similarity between the two in which we are here interested lies in the difficulty of performance. We all know that it is usually quite difficult to act virtuously—for instance, to pay all of one's debts, and to refrain from talking uncharitably about people who have done something mean. Yet the proper effect of practice in virtuous action is precisely to remove the difficulty, so that when virtue is possessed in a state of excellence it is the action contrary to virtue, rather than the virtuous action, that proves difficult. Though their number may not be large, there are people who simply hate to reveal anything that might hurt the reputation of their neighbor. Even when it might be necessary to do so under extraordinary circumstances, they hesitate because it is so contrary to the first of all virtues—

charity. Now what about work? Irksomeness cannot be included in the definition of work for the same reason that it cannot be included in the definition of virtue. Just as the most virtuous person no longer experiences difficulty in doing what is right and would rather find it hard to do the opposite, so the best worker no longer experiences irksomeness in work but perhaps even pleasure. Including irksomeness in the formal definition of work would lead to what is obviously an absurd position—namely, that what the most capable worker does is no longer work. The overwhelmingly common association of work with strenuous effort must mean something, but it cannot mean that pain is an essential characteristic of work.

To pursue this matter further, let us look at a few examples from the literature on work. For instance, one contemporary author urges us to consider a man engaged in playing chess on one occasion and hanging window screens on another. The man is said to be *working* in both instances, "since work is but the exertion of effort towards the accomplishment of a set purpose." The writer continues:

Nevertheless, working at chess is play, while working with the screens is labor. From hours of strenuous concentration on chess, [a man] arises tired but happy. But the exertion of protecting the house against insects leaves him weary, if not also grumpy. The difference between the two occupations is not in the work done, but in that of freedom versus compulsion, which is also the difference between happiness and misery. The screens had to be hung in self-defense; but playing chess was a free choice. Because the motive for play is inner, the work is self-expressive and also self-realizing. The player seeks to improve his game, and as he grows in skill, he is growing in happiness. So the chess player boasts of his game, but the screen hanger bemoans his lot.[16]

[16] Max Shoen, "The Basis for Faith in Democracy," in *Science, Philosophy, and Religion: Second Symposium* (New York: Conference on Science, Philosophy, and Religion in Their Relations to the Democratic Way of Life, 1942), p. 104.

I have indulged in this lengthy quotation because it so well expresses the common notions about work, labor, play, pain, and pleasure. Yet to "act in self-defense" does not always have to be an entirely miserable condition. In the example given, it may conceivably not be unpleasant to hang screens when one is happy that, at long last, the winter is over. Of course, this also means that the insects are coming; but as long as a man is in good health and not tired he may even enjoy the exercise. The difference between playing chess and hanging screens thus does not have to be that between happiness and misery, even if in some sense it may be one of "freedom versus compulsion."

That irksomeness is not essential to work has been ably argued by Thorstein Veblen in his famous essay on the instinct of workmanship. Man's advantage over other species in the struggle for survival, according to Veblen, is his superior facility in controlling his environment. Thus work, in Veblen's words, is "not a proclivity to effort, but to achievement—to the compassing of an end." [17] Veblen also points out that distastefulness and even physical irksomeness of an activity are decisively modified by the context in which this activity is placed by society, as can be seen in attitudes toward warfare:

The most commonplace recital of a campaigner's experience carries a sweeping suggestion of privation, exposure, fatigue, vermin, squalor, sickness, and loathsome death; the incidents and accessories of war are said to be unsavory, unsightly, unwholesome beyond the power of words; yet warfare is an attractive employment . . . both to the barbarian and to the civilized youth.[18]

And from the fact that still other employments distinguished

---

[17] "The Instinct of Workmanship and the Irksomeness of Labor," in *Essays in Our Changing Order* (New York: Viking, 1934), pp. 80–81.
[18] *Ibid.*, p. 95.

from work—such as government, religious observances, and sports—while often distressing are yet always creditable, Veblen concludes that ultimately irksomeness of work is but a socio-cultural phenomenon.[19]

This, however, is not the opinion of Henry De Man. In his *Joy in Work*, De Man does not say that work must of necessity be painful, which would certainly be ironical considering the title of his work. But this intelligent observer of work, who obviously wants to help the working people achieve as much pleasure in work as possible, firmly believes that work always restricts human freedom. According to De Man, association of work with irksomeness is not just a legacy from the days when the social subordination of the worker made work degrading. Even workers who are socially free remain coerced, while at work, precisely by their work. De Man points out that even without a complete overhaul of present social relations, general working conditions could always be made more pleasant and rewarding. But he also points out that the actual working conditions must remain in many respects the same whether carried out under capitalism or under socialism. For De Man this is so because "work inevitably signifies subordination of the worker to remoter aims, felt to be necessary, and therefore involving a renunciation of the freedoms and the enjoyments of the present for the sake of a future advantage." Summing it all up, he writes:

[19] "Physical irksomeness is an incommodity which men habitually make light of if it is not reinforced by the sanction of decorum; but it is otherwise with the spiritual irksomeness of such labor as is condemned by polite usage. That is a cultural fact. There is no remedy for this kind of irksomeness, short of a subversion of that cultural structure on which our canons of decency rest. Appeal may of course be made to taste and conscience to set aside the conventional aversion to labor; such an appeal is made from time to time by well-meaning and sanguine persons, and some fitful results have been achieved in that way. But the commonplace, common-sense man is bound by the deliverances of common-sense decorum on this head—the heritage of an unbroken cultural line of descent that runs back to the beginning" (*Ibid.*, 96). This essay appeared originally in *The American Journal of Sociology*, 4 (September, 1898).

Every worker is simultaneously creator and slave. He is the latter, even if he be the happiest of creators, for he is the slave of his own creation. Freedom of creation and compulsion of performance, ruling and being ruled, command and obedience, functioning as subjects and functioning as objects—these are the poles of a tension which is immanent in the very nature of work.[20]

Without unduly multiplying citations from literature, let us say that, while there are writers who do not believe that work must always be irksome, all who have concerned themselves with the problem of work agree that in one sense or another work involves what they variously call compulsion, coercion, subjection, necessity. They all agree that work is something very serious, regardless of the social conditions of the worker.[21] But while it is universally recognized, this feature of work is seldom explained adequately, and its many names seem only to perpetuate confusion. Personally, I think that this aspect of work should be called *legal fulfillment*. Though I have had many discussions about it, I have decided to keep this term because it seems to me that it describes most objectively what is actually involved in work. But I need to pause here to explain my terms.

Whether or not we are interested in work and the definition of work, we should know that there are, in general, two kinds of human activities. Some activities embody the idea of compliance with a law, while others are thought to be free. For the first type, I have coined the expression *activities of*

---

[20] *Joy in Work*, trans. Eden and Cedar Paul (London: Allen & Unwin, 1929), p. 67. This book was first published in German under the title *Der Kampf um die Arbeitsfreude* (Jena: Diedrichs, 1927).

[21] For instance, Adriano Tilgher writes: "Does an action take itself and its result seriously? This is Work. Does the Action laugh about itself and its result?" This is Sport" (*Work: What It Has Meant to Man through the Ages*, trans. Dorothy Fisher [New York: Harcourt, Brace, 1930], p. 128). The original book by Tilgher (1887–1941) was published under the title *Homo Faber: Storia del concetto di lavoro nella civiltà occidentale* (Rome: Libreria di Scienze e lettere, 1929).

legal fulfillment, in which the adjective "legal" refers not to a statute but to law in the broadest possible sense. I call the second type *activities of free development.* After we have considered a few examples, both these expressions should become more familiar even if not completely clear. There is no denying that these things are profoundly mysterious. Indeed, if we could make these contrasting notions of legal fulfillment and free development completely clear, we would have under control a good deal of metaphysics, a lot of psychology, and almost the whole of ethics.[22]

Let our first example be the following. On a winter day, I enter a coffee shop and order tea, as hot as possible, with the idea that this may be enough to prevent the common disease called "cold." That is a case of legal fulfillment, for there is involved here a natural law relative to the health of the human organism. When this organism has been exposed to cold, experience shows that a good way of preventing further disorder is to put into it something hot (true or not, this seems to be established by experience). Or, I may meet an old friend in the street in any season. I know that he never drinks whiskey, wine, or even beer, and so we step into a coffee shop for a cup of tea. We do this not only in order to have an excuse to be sitting there, but because it is pleasant to drink something while talking and relating stories about the past. That is a case of free expansion. Notice that we have here two activities which so far as nature is concerned are identical. In both cases, some dry leaves of a plant called tea are placed for a few minutes in boiling water and some sugar and lemon are added. But humanly, morally, and socially there is a difference. In one instance, I do something that I have to do in order to protect my health against throat-and-lung infection. In the other instance, neither I nor my friend

[22] See Yves R. Simon, *Freedom of Choice,* ed. Peter Wolff (New York: Fordham University Press, 1969).

needs a cup of tea; but we enjoy each other's company, and a hot drink contributes something to this enjoyment; we enjoy it over and above any need. This is a rather simple example of legal fulfillment contrasted with free development, but the simplest is often the most significant.[23]

Looking for an illustration of this contrast involving actual work, here is a striking example: In *The House of the Seven Gables*, Hawthorne writes: "The life of the long and busy day . . . had been made pleasant, and even lovely, by the spontaneous grace with which these homely duties seem to bloom out of her character. . . . So that labor, while she dealt with it, had the easy flexible charm of play. Angels do not toil, but their good works grow out of them; and so did Phoebe's." [24] Now whether such extraordinarily gifted ladies who can work as others play exist or not, what a nice way to say that activities which ordinarily would be of legal fulfillment have become those of free development!

My third example relates not to manual work but to what we have called intellectual work. It is also a significant illustration of historical and social views on what does and does not constitute work. In Pascal's *Pensées*, there is the famous passage on how Plato and Aristotle are always represented as serious scholars, literally, "dressed in the gown of pedantic

---

[23] Here are a few additional examples. To take a walk after eating to help digestion: legal fulfillment. To take a walk when one will, or when one can, in order to enjoy the landscape, air, and movement: free expansion. I cultivate my garden to produce vegetables for my family: legal fulfillment. I cultivate my garden because I find, in doing so, an interesting and agreeable exercise: free expansion. A young girl practices piano two hours a day according to the program imposed on her by her mother: legal fulfillment. She sits down at the piano to play the tune she loves: free expansion. I read a novel to increase my vocabulary as a writer: legal fulfillment. I read a novel so that I might forget my cares for a while and find an image of happiness: free expansion. From Yves R. Simon, "Work and Workman: A Philosophical and Sociological Inquiry," *The Review of Politics*, 2, No. 1 (January 1940), 63–86.

[24] Nathaniel Hawthorne, *The House of the Seven Gables* (New York: Standard Book, 1931), p. 61.

people." [25] Pascal scoffs at this representation and insists that they were not like that at all. Plato, according to Pascal, wrote his dialogues in about the same way in which Hawthorne says Phoebe kept her house, with all the charm of naturalness and fancy. But to understand what Pascal really meant, we must recall the cultural ideal of the second half of the seventeenth century. This ideal is embodied in the expression *honnête homme*, which in modern French could mean an honest man, but which in the language of the time had no ethical reference. In the seventeenth century this term designated a gentleman of the leisure class, a gentleman who enjoys leisure made beautiful by culture, who appreciates art and even dabbles in it, but who, whatever he does, never has to toil at it. If it strikes his fancy, he may produce a work of art, but he will not need to make any effort to do so.[26] What Pascal is saying, then, is that Aristotle and Plato were *des honnêtes gens*—gentlemen of culture and leisure who, rather than working at their philosophies, wrote their dialogues and treatises just as cultured men of leisure and high society make conversation. Of course, I disagree with Pascal on this. But he has given us here a powerful example of the contrast between the notion of legal fulfillment and that of free development, and he has provided us with an important illustration of the historical opposition between work and culture.

We may take our last example from among the ideas and ideals that inspired the socialist movements of the nineteenth century, and which probably have had a greater influence than is commonly realized on both the thinking and the so-

[25] Fragment 331 (New York: Modern Library, 1941, p. 112).

[26] Léon Brunschvicg has the following note in *Pensées et opuscules* (Paris: Hachette, n.d.; p. 116): "L'honnête homme est à sa place partout; il s'acquitte de tout avec une superiorité qui n'a rien de technique et de contraint, qui est toujours naturelle et aisée; rien en lui ne sent le métier: métier et honnêteté sont choses incompatibles et contradictoires; il ne faut pas même affecter d'être honnête homme; car ce serait en faire une espèce de métier."

cial practices of the twentieth century. For instance, not every historian would include Charles Fourier (1772–1837) with the main founders of modern socialism, even though Marx himself lists him as a utopian socialist. But whether he is classified as a socialist or not, there is no question that Fourier is a utopian of the typical nineteenth-century variety. Above all else, Fourier firmly believes in the principle of harmony. After the fashion of the times, he divides the history of mankind into several distinct periods which through "civilization"—the contemporary stage—lead to an "age of harmony." In this new age, society would be so arranged as to allow human inclinations which in all previous history had been harmful and disruptive of the social order to be harnessed in support of that order.[27]

In this vision of Fourier's, we find in a state of wonderful uninhibitedness and frankness an idea which is present in varying degrees in all modern social science as well as in socialism. For instance, we are all convinced today that an indefinite amount of suffering is inflicted upon mankind merely by poor social organization. But what is characteristic of Fourier is that he turns this idea into an absolute. Thus what he wants to do is no less than satisfy all human appetites (of which he counted about 800) simply by a skillful arrangement of social relations. Because his plan involves the grouping of people into collective units, he is often counted as a socialist. Yet Fourier does not reject private property, either in theory or in his imaginary new social practice. Fourier's

---

[27] Fourier's general theory is perhaps best explained in his *Le Nouveau monde industriel et sociétaire ou invention du procédé d'industrie attrayante et naturelle distribuée en séries passionnées*. This book is the sixth volume of Oeuvres complètes de Ch. Fourier (Paris: Librairie sociétaire, 1845–1846), recently reproduced by Édition Antropos (Paris, 1966). But see also his *Théorie des quatre mouvements et des destinées générales*, and *Théorie de l'unité universelle*, which constitute the first and the third volume of the Oeuvres complètes.

invention is the "phalanstery," a new social entity, the name for which he gets from "phalanx" and "monastery." [28] It is in this new social unit that Fourier expects to see the solution of all social problems, and even of the metaphysical problem of evil. The phalanstery is to contain a number of families, about fifteen hundred people, but there are to be phalansteries also for those who prefer polygamy.[29] In fact, by clever organization and management, all kinds of tastes and preferences could be satisfied there. For example, some people like their bread crusty, others do not. Now, a mother cooking for a single family cannot bake bread in a dozen different ways for a dozen tastes. In the phalanstery, however, all one has to do is establish a system: some of the loaves are taken out of the oven after twenty minutes, some after twenty-five, and so on. Thus particular whims that would be unbearable under present circumstances of social life could be fully satisfied in the new system of phalansteries without much ado.

This roughly illustrates Fourier's general idea of social harmony through social organization. But Fourier has contributed to modernity something even more important. He has given us the theory of *le travail attrayant*, the ideal of work made attractive. In this respect, Fourier has had an immense influence in the development not only of socialism but of every modern inquiry concerned with man at work. The bourgeoisie who made the French Revolution, for instance, had a very gloomy view of work and were convinced that

[28] Fourier justified his neologisms on the grounds that his was a new science. Here are a few other of his terms: "*Séristère, nom des salles et pièces contiguës servant aux séances d'une Série passionnée; Garantisme, Sociantisme, Harmonisme, noms des trois périodes sociales qui succèdent à la cinquième, dite civilisation; Gastrosophie, la gastronomie appliquée à l'attraction industrielle et à l'hygiène; Unitéisme, passion de l'unité, inconnue des civilisés*" (*Ibid.*, Vol. 6, p. v).

[29] In the Introduction to the Édition Antropos reissue of Oeuvres complètes, S. Debout Oleszkiewicz notes that Fourier catalogued nine degrees of adultery and seventy-two kinds of adulterers and adulteresses in "civilized" society.

without suffering, hunger, poverty, and need, it would never be possible to get people to do the dangerous and dirty work which had to be done. Before Fourier, it was widely believed that unless the working class is crushed—by means of freedom of choice between the wage offered in the labor market and starvation—socially necessary work would be left undone. It is to Fourier's credit to have done something to show that the situation is really not that bad, that the life of the worker does not have necessarily to be miserable, and that it should not be necessary to keep the working class in bondage forever. The best known of Fourier's examples of how to make all work attractive is that of clean-up gangs. Since it appears that some little boys are never so happy as when they can play in filth, one has simply to organize a working gang of appropriate ages and tastes. They will find their happiness in tasks which must be performed for the benefit of society, but which everyone else considers disgusting.[30] And so, once again, if suitably organized, everyone can be satisfied simply by being assigned his appropriate place in the social organization.

We perhaps cannot take such simple plans too seriously today, but utopias like Fourier's have been extremely significant historical forces. The fact that this idea of *travail attrayant* was presented by a person quite likely insane, in an unreadable book, did not prevent social thinkers of genius from taking it up. Thus Marx himself owes a great deal to Fourier. While in his plan it is the abolition of private property rather than the establishment of phalansteries which is expected to bring about perfect social harmony, Marx too expects work to be easy and pleasant in his ideal society. In *The German Ideology* (1846), Marx and Engels identify

---

[30] "Parmi les enfants on trouve environ deux tiers de garçons qui inclinent à la saleté. . . . Ces enfants s'enrôlent aux petites hordes dont l'emploi est d'exercer, par point d'honneur et avec intrepidité, tout travail répugnant qui avilirait une classe d'ouvriers" (*Ibid.*, Vol. 6, p. 206).

private property with division of labor and offer a compli-
cated argument about how the forces of production, the state
of society, and individual consciousness can be prevented
from coming into contradiction with each other (causing
alienation). According to their argument, the only way to do
this is through "the negation of the division of labor." What
this means is not completely clear, and Engels himself later
admitted that their "semi-Hegelian language" was untrans-
latable, if not unintelligible.[31] But that difficulty certainly has
not affected the continuing popularity of the idea. Indeed, its
appeal is by no means restricted to the followers of Marx and
Engels. Many have dreamed and continue to dream about a
society in which work itself would be abolished, or at least reduced to a kind of play. According to Marx and Engels, this
is to come about in the following manner:

[In pre-communist society] each man has a particular, exclusive
sphere of activity which is forced upon him and from which he
cannot escape. He is a hunter, a fisherman, a shepherd, or a critical critic, and must remain so if he does not want to lose his means
of livelihood; while in the communist society, where nobody has
one exclusive sphere of activity but each can become accomplished in any branch he wishes, society regulates the general production and thus makes it possible for me to do one thing today
and another tomorrow, to hunt in the morning, fish in the afternoon, rear cattle in the evening, criticize after dinner, just as I have
a mind, without ever becoming hunter, fisherman, shepherd or
critic.[32]

Now let us try to understand exactly what Marx and Engels
are saying. Along the line of thought started by Fourier, they

[31] In a letter to Mrs. Florence Kelley Wischnewetzky, February 25, 1886,
cited in *Marx and Engels: Basic Writings on Politics and Philosophy*, ed.
Lewis S. Feuer (New York: Doubleday, 1959), p. 246.
[32] *Ibid.*, p. 254. Many years later, Marx wrote in the third volume of *Das
Kapital*, Chapter 48: "Das Reich der Freiheit beginnt in der Tat erst da, wo
das Arbeiten . . . aufhört." Cited by Arendt, *The Human Condition*, p. 87n.

clearly maintain something more than simply that by a wiser social arrangement much human suffering could be eliminated and human work made more pleasant. Together with Fourier, they seem actually to expect that under certain specified social circumstances the very irksomeness of work will completely wither away and that work will no longer be work. Translated into our terms, then, what Marx and Engels are saying is that work, in the last analysis, is not an activity of legal fulfillment but rather an activity of free development. And they imagine that in the new society the new man will work in the manner in which Pascal imagined Plato and Aristotle to have philosophized.

If we must disagree again, this does not imply that Fourier and Marx have not made certain important contributions to our understanding of mankind's experience at work, any more than our disagreement with Pascal means that he has not illuminated our understanding of man's intellectual experiences. In regard to work, I myself insist, first of all, that it cannot be fully defined without reference to society; an intelligible definition of work must have a social component. Moreover, I also deny that irksomeness should be included in the theoretical definition of work; irksomeness is not essential to the human activity called work. But on this crucial point my view remains unshakable: work is not, and it can never be, an activity of free development.

Work is by essence a serious activity not only because it is something that has to be done, whether in joy or in sorrow, but also because it is something that has to be done in a way which is largely predetermined. For instance, not only must sewers be cleaned, houses kept, and food gathered or produced in order that men may live; all these things have to be done also according to laws of their own—say, of hydrodynamics, mechanics, chemistry, biology, and so on (and here it does not matter whether these laws are recognized in theory or just empirically). In all cases, man while working deals with things according to their own laws. Now, some writers describe this aspect of work by using such terms as "constraint" and "compulsion." I prefer the term "legal fulfillment," because this seems a more objective name for what happens—when, for example, in building a vault the stonemason obeys the law of gravity. Besides, I do not have to look for another term when I want to show that scientists and philosophers spend a good deal of their time working—that is, in activities of legal fulfillment. Scientific research, including philosophical research, is such an activity—it is definitely work. But should we say that a scientist doing pure research is being "constrained"? This sounds rather awkward. Yet, if he is thought to be free of any constraint, is he still working? [33] My terms avoid such semantic difficulties. I can say that while doing their research scientists and philosophers are working, because I define work not as any kind of "compulsion" but as an activity of legal fulfillment. This usage is also consistent with my position that work does not have to be irksome. Nevertheless, since work is an activity always to a large extent governed by laws which the worker has no power to change, we must all acknowledge that there exists in work a permanent foundation for irksomeness.

[33] The perplexing confusion of popular views on work and the nature of scientific inquiry is strikingly illustrated by the following explanation of pure research by a famous rocket-builder: "Basic research is when I am doing what I don't know what I am doing" (from an interview with Wernher von Braun in the *New York Times*, December 16, 1957).

2

Work and Society

WE HAVE CONSIDERED WORK primarily as an activity of an individual. Let us now see in more detail how much the concept of work depends on man's essentially social nature. There are human activities besides hobbies, exercises, and make-work, already mentioned, which, though they fully satisfy the metaphysical definition of work, simply are not work in actual social contexts. For instance, the activity of a burglar digging a hole in a wall is not work. In saying that burglars do not like to be disturbed when they are at work, the word "work" is used with obvious irony. Burglars do not work. In fact, we think that they are doing something that is the exact opposite of work. Or consider the situation of two brothers, one of whom has decided to get rich by any means, foul or fair, while the other, though not indifferent to financial success, is determined to stick to hard work. This hard work, of course, does not have to be manual labor to qualify socially as work. But getting rich by any means might well involve activities which we would not consider to be work. In a word, what both these examples reveal is that, in order to qualify socially as work, an activity must also be honest. But beyond honesty, there is still another social qualification of work which is somewhat more difficult to explain.

SERVICE TO SOCIETY

I should like to begin by saying that an honest activity, accepted by society, may still not be work of any description if it is unproductive. Specifically, I maintain that operations called speculation are not work, even though they may be both legal and morally acceptable. To avoid misunderstanding, let me repeat: an activity does not have to be immoral in order to be undesirable. The decisive factor here is that we would not want the kind of operations we are talking about to become too frequent. For example, I know of an actual case in which a man had bought a tract of desert land for $4.00 per acre and thirty years later sold it for $1,700.00 per lot, with at least two lots per acre. Such deals have not been uncommon in the Southwest United States. Again, there is nothing vicious about it, and one cannot really blame the man for being smart enough to guess thirty years ago that this desert land, good for nothing and selling for a song, might some day sell for much more. If he bought ten acres, the worst that could ever happen to him would be to lose forty dollars. So he invested his money, and today that land is a wealthy suburb of Phoenix or Albuquerque. Everybody is happy. But is it desirable that these things should occur regularly? Should they be encouraged? I do not think so, because such activities are basically unproductive. True, the man has done nothing, literally—no wrong and no work. But precisely because no work was involved in this operation, a few thousand dollars simply leaked out of society.

The condemnation of commerce in Aristotle and reservations about commerce (*negotium*) in medieval theology refer specifically to operations consisting of a purchase at a lower price followed by a sale at a higher price, without any utility being produced in the meantime.[1] Now, commerce is predicated also of the operation of buying oranges and grapefruit in Florida and selling them in Chicago, but this includes the considerable service of bringing vitamins in the winter to people who are almost snowbound in that dreadful climate. Here is a distinct production of service, and if the compensation of the merchant is about equal to that service, this is not commerce in the sense of Aristotle. Is it work? What does it mean to go to the orchards of Florida or Israel to purchase these crops and to see that they are delivered where needed? The answer is that it is an obvious service, and insofar as the compensation does not exceed the value of that service such an activity is socially productive. The man performing this service is thus not a merchant in the sense of Aristotle, medieval theology, or canon law. He is a producer of "space utility," as the economists call it, and there is no reason why he should be purely and simply excluded from the society of workers. The mark of a true speculator is that he produces absolutely nothing. In our example, he first by purchase effects a legal

[1] For example, "There are two sorts of wealth-getting, as I have said; one is a part of household management, the other is retail trade; the former necessary and honorable, while that which consists in exchange is justly censured" (*Politics* 1258A37–1258B2). See also *Summa Theologica* IIa IIae, q. 77, a. 1, "On Fraud Committed in Buying and Selling": "We next have to consider the sins which have to do with voluntary exchanges. . . . [T]here are four points to be considered: 1.) sales unjust with respect to price, that is, whether it is lawful to sell a thing for more than it is worth; 2.) sales unjust with respect to the thing sold; 3.) whether a seller is bound to point out a defect in the thing sold; 4.) whether it is lawful to sell a thing in trade for more than was paid for it."

transfer of property, and then by sale at the market price thirty years later effects another legal transfer of property. The land of which that property consists was desert, and it has remained desert. One cannot even say that the man conserved the land, for he did absolutely nothing to it; he simply waited for the city to expand in the right direction.

A few years ago, when in a seminar discussion I dared to speak of these things before a couple of economists, one of them immediately said that there was no such operation as a pure purchase, a pure waiting, and a pure sale at a higher price. Indeed, if they do not find a type absolutely prepared in experience some people readily conclude that it does not exist; they do not seem to appreciate that one has to use abstraction to identify an intelligible type. Such tedious experience of idle discussions makes it necessary for us to elaborate on this point.[2] Economic subjects in our time lend themselves so nicely to rhetoric and dogmatism that people who would not fail to grasp the meaning of an abstraction, say, in chemistry, can talk indefinitely to demonstrate that they have not understood the meaning of an ideal type in economics. When a physician says that some conditions demand a diet free from sodium chloride, he does not imply that the thing contained in the salt shaker is ideally pure sodium chloride; he does not even imply that it is in the power of any chemist to isolate one gram of NaCl without any admixture of any other chemical; all that he implies is that there is a relation between the ingestion of a chemical essence symbolized by NaCl and the evolution of a disease, so that, insofar as the patient ingests NaCl, whether in a pure form or in mixture, he can expect to undergo such and such symptoms. Now, when the centuries-old definition of commerce just recalled is voiced in certain circles, it is tempestuously objected that a merchant

[2] See Yves R. Simon, *Philosophy of Democratic Government* (Chicago: University of Chicago Press, 1951; Phoenix Edition, 1961), pp. 237–41.

patterned after this definition is a mythical character impossible to find in the world of experience. It is argued that between the purchase and the sale the merchant produces space utility or time utility (e.g., by keeping it in his basement, he transforms new wine into old). If it were not for the literary habits of thought commonly exercised on such topics, it would be clear to everybody that *insofar* as a man creates space utility by moving a commodity from a place where it is plentiful to a place where it is scarce, or time utility by, in our example, aging wine, he is not a merchant. The relevant question is this: Over and above compensations obtained for such services, is there such a thing as compensation corresponding to no production whatsoever but merely to an advantageous difference between price at the time of the purchase and price at the time of the sale? If such a thing exists, speculation exists and is definable, and the description of its laws is relevant both in a theoretical and in a practical sense, whether or not there exist individuals specialized in speculation and determined not to produce any utility under any circumstances.

The economists I was talking with did eventually agree that pure speculation might perhaps be possible in land, and they added that that was probably the only case. Having elaborated our position, however, we shall use in our discussion not the example of the land speculator but the pure speculator as a type, just as a chemist uses the abstraction called NaCl without having to decide whether or not it is possible to realize this abstraction in a state of absolute purity. Our method thus explained, let us consider the relation of the speculator to society, and let us then decide whether or not what he does is socially productive.

First, let us consider the speculator in the exercise of individual acts of buying and selling. Provided that the rules of the game are observed—i.e., provided that the market has not been sophisticated in any way—all the transactions appear to be absolutely honest. For all we know, the money this man pays for anything he buys is what the thing is worth when he buys it, and the money he receives for anything he sells is what the thing is worth when he sells it. Secondly, however, we must consider the speculator also in his general relation to society. We imagine him close to retirement after a life characterized by skill as well as honesty. He has never indulged in practices designed to influence the market, but he has been so skillful and so lucky in his innumerable transactions that on balance he has gained much more than he lost. Thus his fortune has been acquired by a long series of operations, each of which was absolutely fair and honest. But assuming that he had been a pure speculator—that is, a pure merchant and not a producer of any utility—it is plain that, when his career is considered as a whole, there has been between this honest man and society no real exchange. All the wealth went one way.[3]

In this abstract example, we can see how, through a succession of actions each of which is entirely lawful, wealth can leak out of society. But what happens most clearly in the case of the pure speculator happens to a lesser extent also in the case of the mixed type whose income is part compensation for his services as a producer of some utility and part speculative gain. The important point is that in all speculation, as defined, wealth leaks out of society through operations each of which is perfectly legal and even morally acceptable. Moreover, the market system makes for a permanent possibility of such a leak, and if speculation and activities tending to speculation multiply, burglars, robbers, and swindlers will not be needed to cause social bankruptcy—the regular and perfectly honest operations of the system will suffice.

Let us dare spell it out: the man who does nothing but

[3] See Yves R. Simon, *Community of the Free* (New York: Holt, 1947), pp. 160–165.

speculate—that is, who does nothing but buy and sell—does not work because he does not render a service to society. To qualify as work, an activity must not only be honest but also socially productive. To avoid misunderstanding, as well as the charge of dogmatism, let us again grant that "commerce," in current usage, may well be a necessary component in the system of division of labor in society. But let us also notice that even in this usage—that is, understood not as pure speculation but as a productive activity—everyone recognizes that there can be too much of it and that then it is not good for society. Thus while commerce, even vigorous commerce, may be conducive to social development and betterment, the moment commerce turns into "commercialism" the social benefits derived from it tend to diminish rapidly. Notice that even in our "business culture" such terms as "speculator," "operator," and "wheeler-dealer" are not particularly complimentary, and how much more contumelious they become as antonyms of "honest worker" or "hard worker." Because the speculator tries so hard to "make money," we sometimes fail to see him as completely unproductive—that is, a non-worker. But common sense does not give up so easily, and the frequent complaints about the people who make all the money while others do all the work point directly to the truth of the matter: only socially productive activities qualify to be called work.

THE ETHICS OF THE WORKER

The economists' staunch denial that there can ever be such a thing as pure speculation is derived, interestingly enough, from a source that has also inspired various socialist proposals for the reorganization of society intended to eliminate all possibility of speculation. For instance, on May 17, 1846, Pierre Joseph Proudhon (1809–1865) answered a letter from a young German doctor of philosophy named Karl Marx, who was asking him to enter into some kind of political association. Marx at that time was 28, Proudhon nearly ten years older and incomparably more important in the socialist movement. In Marx's letter there were some things that did not please Proudhon, in particular a veiled allusion to violent revolution. The hint was not very clear, but Proudhon thought it unmistakable, and he wrote back that though he had once believed in revolution—and though he still respected the idea of it—he no longer agreed that it was the best method of social transformation. The best way to solve the problems and difficulties of the capitalist system, Proudhon explained, was to work out a system of economic relationships which would prevent wealth from leaking out of society. In its simplest form, this idea may be said to represent the beginning and the end of Proudhonian socialism.[4]

The common source of these opposing positions in regard to speculation is what we shall call here the ethic or the ethics of the worker, according to our emphasis on ideas or sentiments. There can be no doubt that these notions and feelings represent one of the most interesting cultural trends in modern times. Their origin can be traced to the rising middle class which carried out the commercial and industrial revolutions between the sixteenth and the nineteenth centuries, at

[4] See *Selected Writings of Pierre-Joseph Proudhon*, ed. Stewart Edwards, trans. Elizabeth Fraser (Garden City, N.Y.: Doubleday, 1969), pp. 150–154. The relevant passage concludes as follows: "In other words, through Political Economy we must turn the theory of Property against Property in such a way as to create what you German socialists call *community* and which for the moment I will only go so far as calling *liberty* or *equality*. Now I think I know the way in which this problem may be very quickly solved. Therefore I would rather burn Property little by little than give it renewed strength by making a Saint Bartholomew's Day of property owners. My next work, which at present is in the middle of being printed, will explain this to you further [*System of Economic Contradictions or the Philosophy of Poverty*]." See also J. Hampden Jackson, *Marx, Proudhon and European Socialism* (New York: Collier, 1962). For Simon's writings on Proudhon, see the index to his Bibliography in the Appendix.

which time these ideas and sentiments were eventually taken over in somewhat modified form by various labor movements. The belief that work is the highest value, the fullest and perhaps the only meaningful form of human activity appears to have been expressed most forcefully in the bourgeois literature of the transitional period. "Work alone is noble," Thomas Carlyle wrote in *Past and Present*, while James Russell Lowell "blessed . . . the horny hands of toil," and Henry Wadsworth Longfellow celebrated *The Village Blacksmith* in these rhymes: "His brow is wet with honest sweat, He earns whate'er he can, And looks the whole world in the face, For he owes not any man." [5] Against this background, it is indeed no wonder that when it consciously came into being the modern working class proclaimed through its own spokesmen that it should be the ruling class. [6]

For our purposes here, the general idea and the sentiment behind this glorification of work may be reduced to the proposition that whoever lives in society owes society a debt which has to be repaid by the continual exercise of socially useful activities. While not unfamiliar, this notion of social debt remains rather vague, and if philosophers are good for anything, it should be for analyzing and clarifying concepts which, no matter how vague, convey something of great significance. That one owes a debt to society may be clearer to a person

---

[5] The full stanza from Lowell's *A Glance Behind the Curtain* reads: "No man is born into the world whose work / Is not born with him; there is always work, / And tools to work withal, for those who will / And blessed are the horny hands of toil." In the same spirit, Angela Morgan wrote in the 1920s in *Work: A Song of Triumph*: "Work! / Thank God for the swing of it, / For the clamoring, hammering ring of it, / Passion of labor daily hurled / On the mighty anvils of the world."

[6] Cf. Hannah Arendt, *The Human Condition*, p. 101: "The sudden rise of labor from the lowest, most despised position to the highest rank, as the most esteemed of all human activities, began when Locke discovered that labor is the source of all property. It followed its course when Adam Smith asserted that labor was the source of all wealth and found its climax in Marx's 'system of labor,' where labor became the source of all productivity and the expression of the very humanity of man."

born into a well-to-do family than to a person born into a destitute family. But in either case it is fairly clear that one cannot be alive and active, healthy, trained, educated, and protected, at least most of the time, without incurring some sort of obligation to society, the proper repayment for which might well be in activities that are socially useful. In the ethic of the worker, this proposition has the rank of the first principle. What are its consequences?

Again, the case of the pure speculator is relatively simple (we leave people who engage in socially harmful actions out of the picture altogether). Like everybody else, such an individual in his lifetime has collected all kinds of services from society. He has been protected by the police, he has used public roads, and he has learned geometry because somebody cared to preserve the works of Euclid and Archimedes. Yet, he has never repaid his debt. According to the ethics of modern times, such an individual is absolutely despicable, and that is why liberal economists deny the existence of pure speculation in their economic theories, while socialist reformers are bent on eliminating all possibility of speculation in social practice.

But what about some other types who may not be paying their debts because they are not engaged in socially productive activities? I have in mind in particular persons answering the description of the contemplative sketched above. This contemplative, it will be recalled, is the only social character whom we have already disqualified from the general category of workers by our initial, metaphysical definition of work. The contemplative cannot be a worker in any sense, because contemplation is the exact opposite of worklike activities. But if he is not working, he cannot be paying any debts. Even if what he does may be something better than work, as he contemplates he does not have society on his mind. Contemplation is an activity of the scientific intellect at the term of successful research, and what the contemplative considers are conclusions which, without being exhaustive, are genuine conclusions because they are true. We may also call him a theorist, which is closer to Aristotle's θεωρός, derived from θεωρεῖν, which here means to look at the truth. According to Aristotle, this is the happy man living the best life.[7] But does he have any excuse for living in modern times?

It must be emphasized that the contemplative has received immensely from society. If he is achieving a peak of human excellence, it is because he has been granted rather exceptional privileges. And yet his proper activity is not of itself socially productive. It is, of course, granted that the contemplative does some good in society. For instance, when he happens to speak he speaks so much better than others; he needs say only a few words in order to be socially very useful. Then there is also the value of the example of rest and of dedication embodied in his life. But all this is factual, not essential. We are asking: Is there a theoretical vindication of the life of the contemplative in the ethic of the worker?

It appears that though there have always remained islands of contemplative life, which might even have spread in the last fifteen years or so, the contemplative as a type has been relatively rare in our busy society. Yet if we consider China, India, and Persia together with the medieval Christian, Jewish, and Moslem world, the practice of contemplation or meditation reveals itself as something rather voluminous in the history of mankind. In all these societies we find men who, like the happy man of Aristotle, are more or less completely withdrawn from society. They may live a solitary eremitical life; but since surviving in solitude is rather difficult, hermits generally tend to congregate. What is really interesting is that

[7] *Ethics* 10.7. *Politics* 7.3.

at these other times and places the contemplatives were not only tolerated but were respected and often maintained by the society that they renounced.

It may be considered somewhat of a paradox that, in the bourgeois industrialist liberal society with all its emphasis on individualism and private rights, there is such an undercurrent of contemptuous resentment of contemplatives, whether philosophic or mystical. Generally they are considered idlers, and the only way in which they could perhaps redeem themselves is by some sort of service to society. But if they just contemplate, there is absolutely no justification for their existence. Our puzzlement becomes even greater when we compare the case of the contemplative with that of the financial speculator. The latter like the former is performing no useful service, he is not paying any debts to society, and he is certainly not a worker. But if a man who plays at the stockmarket is not necessarily considered a dishonest man, why should the contemplative be held up to opprobrium for not paying his debt to society?

It is on this particular issue that we must recognize that the ethic of the worker has serious limitations, and that before it is accepted as a satisfactory system something has to be done in it on the subject of contemplatives. The contemplatives are not workers in either the social or the metaphysical sense of the term. They are not, as contemplatives, useful to society. And yet, these useless people may embody the peak of human excellence. For modern society, this is a very keen problem. In most historic societies, the contemplatives were not much of a problem, because if a man could live there without working, and if his happiness was meditation, he could withdraw into a den to be fed by birds without people being upset about it. But in our society, in which everyone is expected to pay his debt to society in socially useful activities, the contemplative is more often than not considered a parasite. Yet how can a man who is "looking at the truth" be despised? How did we ever get involved in this paradox?

I should like to suggest that the main source of this limitation and weakness in the ethic of the worker is to be found in its tendency to identify useful activity with the exploitation of physical nature for human purposes. And since this tendency is also the key to the understanding of many other aspects pertaining to industrial societies, it is of some importance that we consider its concrete social and historical origins, as well as its influence on the social movements in the last six or seven generations.

USEFUL ACTIVITY AND MODERN SOCIAL THOUGHT

To understand modern times, it is essential to understand the Saint-Simonists. Saint-Simon, born in 1760, was a man of great but undisciplined intelligence, an adventurer without regular training in any field of knowledge. "He is wrong inasmuch as he mistakes himself for a scientist, for a scholar," the celebrated mathematician and statesman Hyppolyte Carnot (1801–1888) said, "He is not one; but I have never known another man with such daring visions." When he was seventeen years old, Saint-Simon fought for American Independence under Lafayette. He then went on through a life of incredible adventures, starting many things, finishing nothing. It has been said that his written work improved considerably whenever he had a secretary of genius, and among his secretaries there were two who qualified, each in his own way. The first was the romantic historian Augustin Thierry (1795–1856), undependable as an historian but important in the history of historiography and in the romantic revival of interest in the Middle Ages. The other, nineteen years old when Saint-Simon hired him, was Auguste Comte (1789–1857), the founder of Positivism. Some suspect that whatever is valuable in the work of Saint-Simon was written by either Thierry or Comte, which is probably true insofar as the finished draft is concerned, because Saint-Simon was unable to finish anything. But this adventurer has played a considerable part in modern history merely by having ideas and by planting them in other people's minds.

In the last months of his life (1825), Saint-Simon was surrounded by a number of eccentrics of great ability before whom he played the role of the "prophet of the new times." [8] Most of these men were current or former students of the École Polytechnique, one of the great institutions founded by the French Revolution, a school of engineers famous for its scientific and theoretical orientation. Rumor has it that the students there had repeatedly wrecked the laboratories and antagonized the school staff because in their theoretical bent of mind they lacked experience with people and even with machines. Indeed, it is not surprising at all that such men were willing to listen with the mathematician's lack of inhibitions to an adventurer with a few new ideas. But what were these ideas?

Some of them at least came from the economists. For example, one of Saint-Simon's basic notions was that man's real calling was the transformation of the earth for the welfare of humanity. This was the time just after the period of great revolutionary and Napoleonic wars, when people were tired of military activities and in the mood to turn to industry. In fact, it was Saint-Simon who popularized the use of the word *industriel* to designate precisely the sort of person whom we call an industrialist; the word did not exist in that usage before his time. But despite these similarities with the ideas of the classical economists, the Saint-Simonists also entertained an idea of social organization entirely foreign to the

[8] See Friedrich A. Hayek, *Counterrevolution of Science* (Glencoe, Ill.: Free Press, 1952), p. 129.

older theory. In order best to secure for mankind the benefits of industry, they did not see how economic activity could be allowed to remain scattered, each entrepreneur following the lure of his greatest profit, as was envisaged especially by the British economic theorists. In sharp opposition to the latter, the Saint-Simonists called for leadership and unity in economic activities, and in this difference of views modern socialism was born.

Let us recall that the Suez Canal was dug by a former Saint-Simonist, Ferdinand de Lesseps, as a realization of a Saint-Simonian dream. The same man attempted to dig the Panama Canal, but the work was interrupted by a financial scandal of huge dimensions, and the construction finally was taken over by the United States Government. In carrying out these great enterprises which affected the destiny of mankind, the Saint-Simonists did not believe that individuals should be allowed to follow their lust for gain; the public interest demanded organization and centralization. This view comprises much of what has remained constant in the historical development of socialism.

For instance, Saint-Simonism is discussed in the *Communist Manifesto* together with the systems of Fourier and Owen under the heading of "Critical-Utopian Socialism and Communism." In defence of their own "scientific socialism," Marx and Engels denounce the utopians especially for not understanding the role of the proletariat in the transformation of modern society, and for substituting the fancies of their imagination for facts and trends which they have not understood. But in other respects, the Critical-Utopian Socialists are praised for their attack upon the fundamental principles of the existing society, and here the debt of Marxism to Saint-Simonism is considerable.[9]

⁹ The passages in the *Manifesto* read: "The founders of these systems see, indeed, the class antagonisms as well as the action of the decomposing ele-

The main point to which I wish to call attention is typical of Saint-Simonism, especially in its early period. Put simply, it is the idea that up to now men have been mostly interested in lording it over other men. Too much human effort has been spent in establishing dominion of man over man, with subsequent exploitation of man by man. Again, it is important to realize that this idea comes in the wake of twenty-five years of furious military activity which had demonstrated the potential of modern organization. In fact, the genius behind Saint-Simonism and behind socialism in general is that of Napoleon. It was Napoleon who demonstrated that it was possible to collect an army of half-a-million men who spoke different languages—many of whom were former enemies— and to move it from one end of the continent to another. And what was Napoleon's secret? Organization. By the sheer power of organization, he was able to take this great mass of mankind all the way to Moscow (that he did not bring them back is another issue). The Saint-Simonists were impressed by such feats at the same time as they deplored them as inhuman waste. Thus the central idea of Saint-Simonism, particularly in its early phase, is the contrast between (a) mili-

-----

ments in the prevailing form of society. But the proletariat, as yet in its infancy, offers to them the spectacle of a class without any historical initiative or any independent political movement. . . . Historical action is to yield to their personal inventive action, historically created conditions of emancipation to fantastic ones, and the gradual, spontaneous class organization of the proletariat to an organization of society specially contrived by these inventors. . . . But these socialist and communist publications contain also a critical element. They attack every principle of existing society. Hence they are full of the most valuable material for the enlightenment of the working class." In *Socialism: Utopian and Scientific* (1880), Engels again gives credit to Saint-Simon for recognizing as early as 1802 that the French Revolution was a class war, "not simply one between nobility and bourgeoisie, but between nobility, bourgeoisie, and the non-possessors," and for declaring in 1816 that politics is the science of production. Saint-Simon's mistake was that though he had great interest in the class that was "the most numerous and the poorest," he reserved for the working bourgeoisie a commanding and economically privileged position vis-à-vis the workers. See *Marx and Engels: Basic Writings on Politics and Philosophy*, pp. 37–38; 74–76.

tary activities whose purpose is the domination of man over man and hence of exploitation of man by man, and (*b*) the activity of man upon physical nature for the benefit of mankind.

It is impossible to repeat too often that man cannot exercise any useful action except his action over things. The action of man over man is always in itself harmful to the human species through the double destruction of energies that it involves. It becomes useful only inasmuch as it is secondary and only helps to exercise a greater action over nature.[10]

This "double destruction" obviously means that, while the man who is acted upon is being destroyed, the one who seeks power over other men also wastes his energy. Accordingly, the Saint-Simonists believed that, with the advantages of the alternative of exploiting nature made clear, the exploitation of man by man was bound to disappear. Of course, if a canal is to be dug, there will have to be leaders, and there will therefore also be men who must take orders; but the purpose of it all would not be to set some men over other men. It would be jointly to serve mankind by exploiting physical nature.[11]

It is in this Saint-Simonist view that we find the strictest identification of socially useful action with what we have dis-

---

[10] From the *Organizateur*, Nov. 1819–Feb. 1820. *Oeuvres de Saint-Simon et d'Enfantin* (Paris: Dentu, 1865–1878), Vol. 20, p. 192.

[11] *Doctrine de Saint-Simon. Exposition. Première Année* (1829), edd. C. Bouglé and Élie Halèvy (Paris: Rivière, 1924), p. 144: "The basis of societies in antiquity was slavery. War was for these people the only way of being supplied with slaves, and consequently with the things capable of satisfying the material needs of life; in these people the strongest were the wealthiest; their industry consisted merely in knowing how to plunder." P. 162: "Material activity is presented in the past by the twofold action of war and industry, in the future by industry alone, since the exploitation of man by man will be replaced by the harmonious action of men over nature." P. 225: "The exploitation of man by man, this is the state of human relations in the past; the exploitation of nature by man associated with man, such is the picture that the future presents."

tinguished in the preceding chapter as *manual* and *technical* work, and it is of special importance to note that this idea also was taken over more or less intact by Marxism. On this subject, the Marxists are the followers of Saint-Simon, even though they may lack the roughness and the simplicity of the originators.

In the history of ideas, I have found a law which says that the early phases of great movements are characterized by a lack of inhibitions. That is why I am so interested in these early phases. The Pre-Socratics, for instance, are fascinating because they are completely free from inhibitions that decent academic people experience every time they have something to say. Having said it, academicians immediately back up a little in order to show that they are not quite so naïve and that they are able to achieve a balanced view. The Pre-Socratics have not reached that stage. For instance, Parmenides holds that Being exists and that non-being does not exist, so that Being is for him one big sphere. Whatever is not that big sphere simply does not exist but belongs to a world of appearances. We may not know exactly what he meant, but the least that can be said is that his expressions are blunt and uninhibited. When Thales says that everything is made of water, he presents us with another example of a thinker who has the courage of his opinion. And finally, in Cratylus we find a completely consistent philosopher: He refused to talk at all, because by the time one utters a sentence the flux of becoming has passed on, and so whatever one says can never correspond to the real state of affairs.[12]

Now if we consider the Marxists of the late nineteenth century, we see that they have become in some respects more sophisticated on the subject of socially useful activities. But

---

[12] Aristotle *Meta.* 1010a13. See also G. S. Kirk and J. E. Raven, *The Pre-Socratic Philosophers* (Cambridge: Cambridge University Press, 1957), pp. 74ff on Thales; pp. 263ff on Parmenides, and pp. 182, 198 on Cratylus.

the early socialists are not afraid of being unpolished and of proclaiming bluntly that men act in two ways and only two. One way leads to the exploitation of man by man and is nothing but waste. Therefore, it is the other, consisting in collective effort aimed at the transformation of physical nature for the service of mankind, that is alone useful.

We must also note that though early Saint-Simonism was rather anarchistic, this did not last long, because all organizers have a passion for authority, especially the engineers. The early nineteenth century had had some experience with machines which ran fairly smoothly, and while they were certainly not as good as machines are today, they were already then much more reliable than men. In this respect, there has been an enormous change even, say, in the last thirty years. To start a car used to be quite a problem. Today our cars still break down more often than we would wish; but the number of miles they go without repair is really very impressive. On a higher level of technological precision, there are many parts of our installations that never get out of order. But men get out of order all the time; it is always the human factor which restricts our expectations. Those Saint-Simonist engineers were very conscious of this problem and reacted to it with a super-Platonic system of centralization of planning and of thought-control. Within a few years, they became a most dogmatic and authoritarian sect. We understand very well how this happened; with their passion for organization and huge teamwork it was inescapable. In our time, and not only in totalitarian states, the patterns of indefectible regularity which constitute the norms of the industrial system have created a new passion for authority for the control of men, who appear to be the only things around that get out of control and out of order.[13]

[13] See Simon, *Philosophy of Democratic Government*, Chapter V, "Democracy and Technology."

These aspirations of Saint-Simonism are echoed faithfully in the famous words of Engels about the new society which would be able "to replace the government of persons by the administration of things." [14] Together with the thought in the previously quoted statement of Saint-Simon about the nature and scope of useful human activity, this expectation expresses the hopes of both early Saint-Simonism and genuine Marxism. Whether the rulers of the Soviet Union today would still contend that all they want to do is to administer things rather than to govern people is a moot question. In twentieth-century Bolshevism, this distinction has been somewhat blurred by the fury of the struggles we know so well. *The State and Revolution* (1916), where this idea is still accepted, is said to have been written by Lenin in order to reassure the leaders of labor unions, among whom the philosophy of anarcho-syndicalism was still prevalent. But in subsequent developments the withering-away of the state was relegated to the inexplorable part of the future, and the distinction between the government of persons and the administration of things has been all but forgotten. It now belongs to the history of socialism in the nineteenth century, the century that ended with the First World War and the Russian Revolution.[15]

[14] *Socialism: Utopian and Scientific*, in *Marx and Engels*, p. 106.

[15] In 1959, Nikita Khrushchev gave the following interpretation of this famous dogma: "Marxism-Leninism teaches us that under communism the state will wither away and that the functions of public administration will no longer have a political character, and will pass under the people's direct administration. But we should not take an oversimplified view of the process. We should not imagine that the withering away of the state will resemble the falling of leaves in autumn, when the trees are left bare. The withering away of the state, if we approach the question dialectically, implies the development of the socialist state into communist public self-administration. For under communism, too, there will remain certain public functions similar to those now performed by the state, but their nature, and the methods by which they will be exercised, will differ from those obtaining in the present stage" (*Control Figures for the Economic Development of the U.S.S.R. for 1959–1965* [Moscow, 1959], p. 123). This was Khrushchev's report to the Twenty-first Party

So much for the European developments. But let us also take it with a grain of salt when we hear it said that the American labor movement is not ideological in character. Even though it certainly is not as doctrinaire as those of Spain or France or Germany, the American labor movement too has had its visions of the society of the future. Samuel Gompers, for instance, was a very astute and practical leader of men and a conservative in many respects. Nevertheless, he too cherished the belief that, when labor came to be sufficiently organized, all really important social problems would be taken care of, so that political government would naturally pass into non-existence.[16] We often read in the documents of the Labor Movement that work or labor (the first if we speak of the activity, the second if we speak of the men who exercise this activity) ought to be supreme in society. At the bottom of this view is the old Saint-Simonist idea that men may

---

Congress. By the time of the next Congress, this dialectical process had produced the expression "the state of the whole people." "The draft Programme of the Party raises, and resolves, a new important question of communist theory and practice—the development of the dictatorship of the working class into a state of the whole people, the character and the tasks of this state, and its future under communism. *The state of the whole people is a new stage in the development of the socialist state, an all-important milestone on the road from socialist statehood to communist public self-government*" ("On the Programme of the C.P.S.U.," in *The Road to Communism* [Moscow, 1962], p. 148; italics in the original).

[16] For instance, in an editorial in the *American Federationist*, August, 1923, p. 624, Gompers wrote: "I have said and I should like to repeat here that political government has definite limitations in the ordering of affairs, and it can go beyond these limitations only at the peril of the people and their social and economic organization. Political government, for example, is simply not competent to conduct industry, to work out the salvation of industry, or to teach industry which paths to walk. There is a great gulf between politics and industry. Industry must work out its own salvation, build up its own great governing forces, apply democratic principles to its own structure and meet the needs of humanity out of its own intelligence." See also his *Seventy Years of Life and Labor*, 2 vols. (New York: Dutton, 1925). A convenient secondary source is Louis S. Reed, *The Labor Philosophy of Samuel Gompers* (New York: Columbia University Press, 1930). On page 127, Reed quotes Gompers as saying: "I still believe with Jefferson that that government is best which governs least."

struggle either to lord it over other men, to exploit them and be served by them, or to control physical nature for the benefit of all mankind. As the former involves a "double destruction," only the latter activity is of any real use to society. All human effort, therefore, should be directed to administration of things.

Again, the broad intention of Socialism is to return to society, either by violent action or by some particular economic scheme, the wealth that leaks out of it under the capitalist system; the moral vision which accompanies these social plans is the ethic of the workers, whose pride it is that through daily activity upon physical nature they pay society back for services rendered. Let us not hesitate to declare openly that recognizing this debt to society represents the glory of the ethical disposition of socialism. But let us at the same time not forget that in this view anything pertaining to political government is judged as being an inferior kind of activity. This too is a characteristic of the ethic of the worker, and its origin must be traced to the view that "socially useful activity"—which is in itself not a bad definition of work—is restricted to action upon physical nature.

This restricted view of socially useful activities is what is really behind the suspicion of politics so prevalent in modern ideologies, liberal as well as socialist. It is also what is behind the resentment of the contemplatives. Now, interestingly enough, the problem of the debt which every individual owes to society is found also in Aristotle, who does not restrict socially useful activity to action upon physical nature. As is well known, the first place among social activities in Aristotle's philosophy is reserved for politics, and for him it is the statesman or the citizen rather than the worker who is considered to be paying his social debt in full. Nevertheless, the decisive standard in both cases is social utility, as Aristotle judges the citizen according to his contribution to the common good. And yet, for Aristotle, the very best life is that of the man who withdraws from society into solitude to contemplate and to keep seeking after truth. Does this mean that Aristotle is inconsistent? Does it mean that, by denying any exceptions for the contemplatives, the modern view on social obligations is more consistent than Aristotle's? I do not think so, for a rather simple reason. Contemplative life can easily be justified in Aristotle's philosophy, because he has an idea of the good that is not merely useful but is better than useful, because it is desirable for itself, because it is an end in itself. Such a notion of the good is absent in much of modern philosophical thought, and that is ultimately why in this thought there is no ground on which to justify the autonomy of science, of philosophy, or even of political activity. Thus when all is said and done, what we have identified above as a major shortcoming of the ethic of the worker, namely, the resentment of the contemplatives, cannot really be overcome without first recognizing the goodness of things that have nothing to do with social utility.[17]

THE SOCIOLOGICAL CONCEPTION OF THE WORKING MAN

We may conclude these remarks on work as a social activity by distinguishing briefly between what I call the socio-ethical and the sociological conceptions of the worker. As mentioned above, some years ago I had proposed a definition of the working man that included only people professionally busy with some action exercised upon physical nature. According to this definition, professional activities ultimately concerned with pure science or with social order were not considered work strictly speaking. This narrow view was sharply criticized by a number of writers,[18] and further reflection on the prob-

[17] *Ethics* 1.7.
[18] See Jose Todoli, o.p., *Filosofia del Trabajo* (Madrid: Instituto social Leon XIII, 1954), pp. 11-15, 20-25.

lem of the definition of work has led me to conclude that at
least some of that criticism was the result of my failure to
distinguish clearly between two points of view which are indeed profoundly distinct from one another: namely, the
socio-ethical and the *sociological*. Here, we must make sure
of that distinction.

Ethics being the science which deals with the order to be
assured by reason in the voluntary actions of man, let us say
that a consideration is relevant to the ethical point of view
when it is dominated by the purpose of discovering the right
order to be established in the uses of human freedom. Accordingly, considerations relevant to the socio-ethical point of
view are those which are dominated by the purpose of establishing the right conduct for the individual in his relations
with members of social groups to which he belongs. From
this point of view, work may be defined simply as an activity
implying a service rendered to society, which confers on the
person performing this service the right to receive an equita-
ble compensation for it. For instance, we all recognize that
statesmen and clergymen, policemen and psychiatrists, perform services useful both to society at large and to individuals, and most of us believe that these people are entitled to
a decent remuneration for their services. And yet, in the current and spontaneous use of words, there is a strong repug-
nance toward designating such persons as judges, soldiers,
members of representative assemblies, or clergymen, teachers
of philosophy, physicians, and the like, as workers, working
men, members of the working or laboring class. We say that
a priest is *working* when he is not resting. We say that like
anyone else who works, he deserves a just salary. But it would
sound strange and even ridiculous to say that he belongs, as
a priest, to the social category called "workers." Thus what
actually happens here is that, in the first instance ("the priest
is working"), we adopt spontaneously a psychological and

metaphysical point of view; in the second instance ("he deserves a just salary"), a socio-ethical point of view; and in the third instance ("he is not a workman"), a sociological point of view.

The nature of sociological science may still be disputed, but the least that can be said without embracing any particular school is that sociology properly so-called is the science which refers to *social causality*—that is, to the causal power of social beings—as the proper principle of its explanations. In other words, the proper effect to be explained by sociology being the social fact *qua* social, and the proper cause to which the sociological explanation makes appeal being the social group as such, a consideration is relevant to the sociological point of view inasmuch as it is formally concerned with some proper effect issued by the causal power of such social beings. Einstein is reputed to have said that when he wanted to elucidate some notion he asked himself in the first place: What does this notion mean to me *as a mathematician?* When we consider the notion of work formally *as sociologists*, the aspect which is predominant for us is the ability of labor-activity to determine a special kind of grouping among men. Such terms as "working classes," "labor groups," and "working section of the society" do not express fictions arbitrarily invented by theorists. They express the factual grouping of men in specific communities, and the sociological definition of the worker is determined by the factual boundaries of such a community. And here we see that, as a matter of fact, social theorists in the most different conditions of time, environment, theoretical principles, and practical aims oppose almost constantly the category of workman not only to the category of idlers, and to the smaller category of wise men, but also to such categories as soldiers, statesmen, judges, and clergymen.

Many classical economists and some contemporary socialists have strongly indicated that they consider statesmen, sol-

diers, and clergymen to be good for nothing.[19] By contrast,
Plato recognizes these people as the most useful to the city.
But no more than these other theorists does he bear in mind
that they might ever be counted among the workmen. Thus
when Veblen describes the working class as "this great body
of people" which in its everyday life is "at work to turn things
to human use," [20] and when in opposition to this working
class he defines as a leisure class those occupied throughout
all history with "government, warfare, religious observances
and sports," [21] he expresses a conception which is most generally accepted among social theorists.

The specifically sociological concept of "the worker," then,
is relatively a narrow one. Letting it appear decisive for an
overall definition of work was a serious flaw in my early position, and it is no wonder that it caused resentment among so
many who did not feel that they should be excluded from the
category of workers. I have since learned a great deal about
moral and social work, about the theoretical features of
manual work as compared to art, and about the psychology of
the worker. From the sociological standpoint, however, I cannot say that my views have changed. I wish to repeat that
being excluded from the sociological category of workers cannot be an insult to anyone, unless it is postulated that the
working man alone is respectable, that he alone has the right
to food rations. Unfortunately, many social movements since
about the end of the eighteenth century have more or less
explicitly embraced precisely such a postulation. It is voiced
uninhibitedly by the Saint-Simonists and echoed in a hundred ways by both conservative and liberal as well as socialist

---

[19] It was Adam Smith who wrote: "The whole, or almost the whole public
revenue, is in most countries employed in maintaining unproductive hands"
(*The Wealth of Nations* [New York: Modern Library, 1937], p. 325).
[20] *Essays in Our Changing Order*, p. 84.
[21] *The Theory of the Leisure Class* (New York: Modern Library, 1934),
p. 2.

champions of industrial life. The pressure which these ideologies exert against an objective inquiry into the place of work in human life and society is very great, and no clarification in these matters is possible without firmest resistance to all ideological influences.

In this resistance, we may take courage from the fact that sociological theory, as distinguished from ideologies, follows a line already traced by our theoretical inquiry into the nature of work. We have seen that, from a metaphysical point of view, manual work is the fullest realization of the idea of work, and sociological investigations confirm that social consciousness designates the manual worker as the archetype of the working man. Correspondingly, the sociological term "working class" designates primarily the class of manual workers, and while it may also refer to people who direct manual work, such as various types of foremen and master craftsmen, it definitely excludes all those who are not concerned with action exercised upon physical nature. Moreover, in a sociological classification of social groups, people engaged in what we have called the works of the mind—technical, social, and purely intellectual work—are placed at distances from the working class corresponding faithfully to the place of their activity on our diagram of the polar opposition between work and contemplation. Thus while these people may be considered workers in several senses, including the socio-ethical, they definitely are not workers in the sociological sense. From the sociological standpoint, the only group considered collectively as workmen is the group whose members are habitually engaged in action upon physical nature.

3

Man at Work

LET US EXAMINE several interesting aspects of work in order
to see how they affect both the individual and society. Specifically, I propose first to compare the worker as a psychological type with certain other psychological types. Secondly,
I propose to compare work considered as a foundation of
sociability with certain other activities which also bring
people together. Thirdly, I propose to consider briefly the
problem of alienation which has been talked about so much
in modern times, but which is certainly not new as far as work
and workers are concerned. The clarification of these matters
will prepare us to take up the historical subject of the working
class discussed in the next chapter.

THE PSYCHOLOGY OF THE WORKER

A man who likes to spend eight hours or more a day doing
some sort of manual work may be considered a worker not

only in metaphysical, socio-ethical, and sociological senses but also in a psychological one. Moreover, all those persons who endlessly enjoy managing factories, projects, schools, towns, or their own families—and who when they retire are as good as dead—are, from a psychological point of view, first of all workers. Even a man dedicated to a life of pure study but constantly struggling toward something new, gathering data, testing hypotheses and discussing them with fellow experts—and who the moment he establishes a truth is off onto something else—also has the psychology of the worker.[1]

In George Bernard Shaw's *Pygmalion*, we find this psychology well expressed in the words of Higgins, who says: "Once for all, understand that I go my way and do my work without caring two-pence what happens to either of us."[2] Clearly, Higgins is not interested in people; he is interested only in his work. But there is more to the psychology of the worker, and perhaps no one put it better than Nietzsche in that famous passage in which Zarathustra, asked about his happiness, replies: "I ceased long ago to strive toward my happiness; I strive for my work."[3] Here, work is not *die Arbeit*, namely the activity, but *das Werk*, that is, the thing to be produced. The worker as a psychological type is concerned exclusively with his *Werk*. His interest is neither in the self, nor in another human being, nor even in an action exercised by

[1] "Psychology" and "psychological" are taken here in their most familiar, least technical sense. When we say of a man of action that he is a good psychologist, or when we describe some novelists or moralists—e.g., Dostoevsky or Confucius or Montaigne—as great psychologists, we mean that they are excellent at understanding the mind and the heart of men considered concretely—that is, in the context of use. This is the point relevant for the purposes of action. In order to foresee how a man is going to behave and how far we can trust him, it *may be relevant* to know about the particularities of his memory and of his sense perception, but the thing *decisive* is how he is inclined to *use* whatever ability he has.

[2] Act 5. *Androcles and the Lion Overruled. Pygmalion* (London: Constable, 1949), p. 290.

[3] Friedrich Nietzsche. *Thus Spake Zarathustra* (New York: Modern Library, 1905), p. 263.

a human subject; his interest is absorbed in a thing strictly external to man.

Thus we may almost say that a man is a worker in the psychological sense when he surrenders his happiness for an object which he fully appreciates as being external and impersonal. From this angle we see again how the contemplative as such can never be a worker even in the psychological sense. True, contemplation also is centered in an object—namely, the objective truth—but obviously this object must be in the human subject before it can be contemplated. And yet, psychologically speaking, the contemplative is not the type whom we should set in contrast to the worker without qualifications. Even though contemplation itself is an immanent action *par excellence*, obtaining the knowledge of truth is a complex and often tedious process of experience and abstraction, analysis and comparison, induction and deduction, so that even in the purest scholarly life the time dedicated to research, which is hard work, outweighs by far the time dedicated to the contemplation of the results of that research.[4] Because the human intellect is not intuitive but discursive—which means that it has to gather its data from sense experience and indirectly from the teaching of others—most of us organize our psychology for the search rather than for the final consideration of what may be found at the term of our inquiries. This practice is not absolutely necessary, but it is more or less inevitable, and it tends to blur the distinction between the contemplative and the worker as psychological types.

To tell the truth, this concentration upon research rather than its results has been an extremely common preference, especially in modern times. In history, it is always imprudent to say "exclusively," but it does seem that the myth of the primacy of research over contemplation has become more

[4] See Yves Simon, *L'ontologie du connaître*, Chapter III, "L'Expérience et la pensée."

popular since the eighteenth century or thereabouts. In fact, this preference has been the characteristic way of thinking for several past generations in not a few parts of the world. The myth itself was brilliantly expressed about two hundred years ago in a polemic by the celebrated eighteenth-century dramatist, philosopher, poet, and literary critic Gotthold Ephraim Lessing (1729–1781), who is perhaps the best-known name of the German Enlightenment. In this article, Lessing tells the story of God offering man what He has in His two hands: one hand holds out the truth without research, and the other holds out research without the slightest hope of ever finding the truth. Lessing naturally chooses research, without the slightest hope of ever finding the truth.[5] I say "naturally" because, had he chosen the truth, he would not have written the piece. Unending research preferred to the truth! I know this spirit best as expressed in modern times, but I would not certify that it did not exist in the Renaissance, in the Middle Ages, or even in antiquity. It is very much a human choice that could appeal to anyone, anytime.

The important thing for us is to make sure that this dedication to never-ending research, which is a radical perversion of the relation of man to truth, be not confused with something which is only an accident—namely, an instrumental psychology organized about research. In the latter case, a man striving toward truth does not in principle subordinate truth to research without results. When he succeeds in grasping a particle of truth, he does not despise it. And yet, within five minutes he will start looking for something else. That is how

---

[5] "Wenn Gott in seiner Rechten alle Wahrheit und in seiner Linken den einzigen, immer regen Trieb nach Wahrheit, obschon mit dem Zusatze, mich immer und ewig zu irren, verschlossen hielte und spräche zu mir: 'Wähle!,' ich fiele ihm mit Demut in seine Linke und sagte: 'Vater gib!, die reine Wahrheit ist ja doch nur für dich allein!' " ("Duplik," in Werner Burkhard, *Schriftwerke deutscher Sprache* [Aarau: Sauerländer, 1946], Vol. 2, p. 103). I wish to thank Professor Douglas F. Bub of the Department of Foreign Languages at the University of South Carolina for this quotation.—Ed.

most of us are, and that is not contemplative psychology. Again, it is difficult to develop a contemplative psychology under circumstances which require so much intellectual work. Though entirely contained within man, intellectual effort is still a kind of work: it is useful, it proceeds by way of motion and change, and it is certainly an activity of legal fulfillment. That is why we rightly call the philosopher who can never relax a hardworking man, an excellent worker. He does not necessarily subordinate truth to research as Lessing does, but he may not be completely free from what even if accidental is still a disorder: his psychology is organized about striving toward truth rather than about the truth itself, with the result that the meaning of the striving will be lost sight of many times. Indeed, psychologically speaking, the potential contemplative (whether a philosopher or a "pure" scientist) is not the type to set in opposition to the worker.

For the sake of being thorough, let us ask next whether we can expect to find the psychology of the worker fostered in moral and social strivings. The answer is not obvious, for it depends upon whether what is striven for is the order of wisdom within myself or the order of wisdom in society. If the striving is toward the order of wisdom within myself, it seems that it can hardly miss the state of rest in the order which is striven for. The accident by which we lose sight of the aim and concentrate on the struggle does not seem to happen so frequently when we strive toward the establishment of moral order within ourselves. But when we are concerned with order in society, the situation changes radically. For all sorts of reasons, the social order is constantly in jeopardy, and the progress achieved this morning is likely to be undone tonight. This is really the difficult aspect of human society. More often than not, when we think that a problem is solved, we are confronted in the next instance by the same problem in a somewhat different shape. And what a situation like that calls for is indeed an endless driving, which would be impossible without the psychology of the worker, but which again involves the danger of losing sight of the end that gives meaning to the whole effort.

We see, then, that both people engaged in intellectual pursuits and people active in society have good reasons to develop, or to succumb to, the psychology of the worker, which we assume is present in its strongest and clearest form in the manual worker. It is a sort of occupational hazard in all three cases. In consequence, philosophers and statesmen, or scientists and policemen, or even priests, cannot be clearly distinguished as psychological types from people who like to work with their hands all day long. But, we may ask, excluding those suffering from sloth, are there any general types that stand in clear opposition to the worker considered as a psychological type? I think that there are at least two. I propose to call them the enjoyer and the lover.

WORK, JOY, AND LOVE

Taking the enjoyer first, let us try to see first of all that joy is an activity beyond motion. True, we all find joy in change, but that is only insofar as it is a sort of accomplishment. It is not *qua* change that change is cause of joy, but *qua* actuality. Under this aspect, change must be seen as that which is aimed at by certain tendencies proper to mutable beings; for as change is the way of actuality proportionate to them, it is in change that they find their joy. But joy as an accomplishment is rest beyond motion and change.[6]

Now, it is certainly not by accident that in the psychology of the people who like to enjoy themselves, intellectually, ethically, or otherwise, we seldom find an obsession with work. If asked about his work and his happiness, an enjoyer would

[6] See Aristotle, *Ethics* 10.4.

say, contrary to Zarathustra, "I work only as is needed for my happiness, which is the thing I am striving for." Notice also that we do not expect to find this kind of psychology, at least not regularly, among either manual workers or engineers. Moreover, as far as scientists and contemplatives are concerned, in order for them to become enjoyers they would have to keep in mind that their research is merely useful and that it is the truth which they are after. Similarly, in moral discipline and community action an enjoyer would always have to be conscious that what he is striving toward is happiness and peace within himself and in society. But here it is also quite clear that the job of the chief of police in New York or Chicago is not one for the enjoyer. In such jobs too much pugnacity is needed, which is a disposition unlikely to be found in a man of whom it is said that he is a charming fellow who likes to enjoy himself.

Turning now to the lover considered as a psychological type, let us first explain that we take love here in the fullest sense of this noble word—that is, in the sense of friendship rather than of covetousness. Though it is a kind of love, the real center of covetousness is my own self. But in the love of friendship the center is another self, and that is why we hold that love is realized more truly in friendship than in covetousness. For instance, when we meet a fellow who is extremely friendly to many people in expectation of the advantages he can obtain from them, we quickly conclude that he has no friends at all, for the simple reason that he really does not love anybody but himself. Thus the true lover is one who loves according to friendship and whose center of interest is in another self.[7]

With this general notion of love in mind, we can see that the manual worker as such has little in common with the lover as a psychological type. I emphasize "manual worker as

[7] See *Ethics* 8.3, 5; 9.12.

such," because a worker may of course ultimately be motivated by love. For instance, a man may work hard to grow vegetables for his family whom he loves dearly. But while he is out working, the center of his activity is neither in himself nor in another self but in the vegetables. The same kind of concern with the things worked on is found in the technician, the engineer, and the architect, all of whom while not themselves necessarily busy with their hands are busy directing manual work. They are all cold-blooded types, as it were, whose principle of operation has been well expressed by Shaw's Higgins in the line from *Pygmalion* quoted above. Indeed, a person with the psychology of the worker can be very ignorant of love and friendship. This is not surprising, for his center of interest is not in persons but in things or, in cases like Higgins', in persons considered as things.

What about the contemplative? Is contemplation a cold-blooded or a warm-blooded operation? We have seen that, psychologically speaking, the intellectual pursuits incline one to develop the psychology of the worker. But perhaps there are circumstances under which the contemplative could develop the psychology of the lover. This is a profound problem, and it may be best to consider first its historical aspects which are extremely interesting.

The contemplative of Aristotle is a scholar who has achieved full control over himself, possesses economic independence, and is at peace with his fellow men. He has achieved such a level of self-sufficiency that he can withdraw, perhaps to the desert, or at least into his studies, and there keep searching until, at long last, he sits down to contemplate the results of his inquiries. There is nothing friendly about this man as a person; his contemplation is in itself strictly an intellectual operation.[8] To describe this activity even as cold-blooded may be an exaggeration; there is life in it but no blood.

[8] See *Ethics* 10.7. *Politics* 7.3.

Now, this may or may not be the highest kind of life obtainable by man, but one thing is certain: we cannot expect much love in it. However, this is only Aristotle's contemplative. If we follow the evolution of ideas and sentiments about contemplation, we encounter after a few generations of Christianity, at the latest, the beginnings of a life of contemplation of another psychological type in whom the contemplative is also a lover. I speak of Christianity because it is the religion and religious sociology that I know best. One would probably find something similar in Jewish, Hindu, or Buddhist mysticism. Yet I have little doubt that the peak of this warm-blooded life of contemplation is achieved by the great Christian mystics, Catherine of Siena in the fourteenth century, Theresa of Avila in the middle of the sixteenth century, and John of the Cross, the most gifted and intellectual, as well as the best writer of them all, who died in 1591 at the age of 55.[9] With these mystics we have something foreign to the Greek wise men, at least of the Aristotelian description. The comparison with Neoplatonism and Plotinus would be another matter, for Plotinus adopted little children from the streets.[10] In this respect, Neoplatonism, although frequently represented by opponents of Christianity, has relations to the Hebrew tradition, to Christianity, and also to the mysticism of the East. So all told, we find the contemplative who is also a lover represented rather abundantly in history. In this type of contemplation, which is essentially relative to persons, it is precisely this relation to persons that constitutes the happiness of the contemplative.[11] We too know this happiness when we say that to love a person is to want to be happy with him.

[9] See John of the Cross, *The Dark Night of the Soul*, trans. Kurt F. Reinhardt (New York: Ungar, 1957).

[10] See A. H. Armstrong, *Plotinus* (London: Allen & Unwin, 1953). See also Emile Bréhier, *The Philosophy of Plotinus*, trans. Joseph Thomas (Chicago: University of Chicago Press, 1958).

[11] See Jacques Maritain, *The Degrees of Knowledge* (New York: Scribners, 1959), Second Part, especially Chapters VIII and IX.

Returning to Aristotle, let us see finally whether there is anything to what Chrysippus has said about the happy man of Aristotle. This man, the Stoic philosopher maintains, far from being above the rest of mankind is as selfish as anyone else, the only difference being that he places his enjoyment in scholarship while others place theirs in the senses. Now, to be sure, the scholar described by Aristotle as leading the best life is a kind of pleasure-seeker; he seeks a state of excellence— namely, the state of intellect in the act of understanding— from which a distinguished pleasure results.[12] A hedonistic interpretation of Aristotle's eudaemonism is thus not entirely implausible. And yet, Aristotle's contemplative cannot be viewed simply as a pleasure-seeker, no matter how ardently he may seek the pleasure of knowing. Among other reasons, this is so primarily because his pleasure results from an activity centered on the truth as an object and demanding total submission to it.[13] In other words, Aristotelian contemplation is a beatitude of the trans-subjective type; it is an objective beatitude. In my opinion, this suffices to exclude all hedonistic interpretation of Aristotelian philosophy. But it does not change the fact that the happiness of Aristotle's contemplative, even though trans-subjective, is not loving.

In conclusion, let us also briefly consider whether moral and social actors have anything in common with the lover as

---

[12] See Emile Bréhier, *Chrysippe* (Paris: Presses Universitaires de France, 1951), Book Two, Chapter III, paragraph one, "Le sage et la fin des biens."

[13] *Meta.* 4.1. "There is a science which investigates being as being and the attributes which belong to this in virtue of its own nature. . . . Now since we are seeking the first principles and the highest causes, clearly there must be some thing to which these belong in virtue of its own nature. If then those who sought the elements of existing things were seeking these same principles, it is necessary that the elements must be elements of being not by accident but just because it *is* being. Therefore it is of being as being that we also must grasp the first causes." See also the Foreword by Yves Simon to *The Material Logic of John of St. Thomas*, trans. Yves R. Simon, John J. Glanville, and G. Donald Hollenhorst (Chicago: University of Chicago Press, 1955).

a psychological type. Here, an affirmative answer seems to be inevitable. Since my own life is essentially social, I do not see very well how I could struggle toward an order of wisdom within myself without simultaneously struggling also toward what is good for my fellow men—that is, without being genuinely interested in other people. It is even clearer that social action in the community at large must be combined with the psychology of the lover if it is to be genuine. We all expect social workers to be animated by love, because when they are not so animated social work is necessarily perverted. How could it be social work, if it is not coupled with love for one's fellow men?

THE SOCIABILITY OF THE WORKER

The foregoing comparison of the worker as a psychological type with the enjoyer and the lover seems to have left the worker in an unflattering light. He is not interested even in himself, let alone in other people; all he is interested in is his work. Thus to speak next of the sociability of the worker may appear as a complete reversal of position. But it is not, and after we have considered this subject at some length, the worker, despite the features in his psychology which we have noticed above, may still emerge as an acceptable, even desirable, social type.

We all know that men form associations on many grounds and for many purposes. Moreover, we all understand that, by virtue of the forms of their associations, people are related to each other in the social whole in definite and particular ways. Now, assuming that the life of work supplies a distinct ground for human association, we want to find out both what that ground is and what constitutes the particular form of association by work. Our discussion should also serve to emphasize the extraordinary importance of the study of all forms of sociability. To say that man is a social and political animal is tantamount to saying that men are shaped by the forms of their sociability, and I cannot think of any more direct way to a better understanding of men and of what society can do for men than through the study of these forms.

We may begin by recognizing that work is a cause of common life of unique significance in regard both to time and to the numbers of people involved. For instance, any one of us may have a few friends sharing, say, a passion for Impressionistic painting. He would then meet occasionally with these friends to have tea, to talk about Impressionistic painting, and to view together the productions of this school. That is very nice. What we have here is a communion in the appreciation of a particular form of art. But while this is wonderful in itself, as a cause of sociability it leaves much to be desired. It not only leaves out uncounted millions of people who do not care about Impressionism, but it also fails to make those few who appreciate Impressionism feel that their group is living within each and all of them at all times. The great advantage of work is that it promotes precisely such feelings and not only among a chosen few but practically among the whole of mankind.

In order to clarify the grounds and the particular form of the sociability of the worker, we should recall that manual work is an external, or transitive, action. Like everyone else, manual workers of course associate for the purpose of achieving a certain common task. But the grounds on which they associate is a transitive, external action, and the ways in which they associate and are related to the social whole cannot be divorced from the nature of such an undertaking. Again, we must always remember that internal actions too provide distinct grounds and ways of sociability, and that there is a significant contrast between association, or union, in a collective external action and union—or better, communion—in an immanent action. For example, why are baseball and football games so important? I do not know all the rules of either baseball or football, but whenever I happened to attend a game I was strongly aware of the communion among thousands of spectators in following whatever was going on. The social value of these Saturday afternoon entertainments should not be underestimated. Their importance is not unlike that which attaches to holiday parades or to the ceremony of saluting the flag, which takes place in all public schools across the country five mornings a week. In all these events and actions, social life attains great profundity and intensity, and they all make us realize how unintelligent it is to describe society as something essentially external to man and to the human soul, as if society were a kind of machinery. What is most social in man takes place inside men in immanent actions of joy, love, or even simple awareness, and the deeper such feelings are in the individual, the more social is the event that we are observing.

Now, to work together in order to build a house, dig a canal, or drain marshes means to be engaged in collective external actions which do not have the same profundity as immanent acts of knowing, enjoying, or loving the same thing together. But while work as a ground of sociability does not have the same profundity, it has something else: it occurs daily and it occupies far more space and time in human life than any other activity. Moreover, in a lofty immanent action there is always something almost superhuman. Consider people who commune in the enjoyment of a great scientific discovery or philosophic achievement. This is relatively rare, since such attainment is above the level of the kind of activity which is entirely proportionate to man. At the beginning of the first book of the *Metaphysics*, Aristotle describes the necessity and the characteristics of a philosophy of first principles, and he remarks that its possession "might be justly regarded as beyond human power." [14] Even though it is the most excellent science, we cannot expect to find it often in a state of excellence, for it is a little too lofty and too difficult for men to practice it, except rarely, in a state of excellence. By contrast, work is definitely the kind of activity proportionate to the balance of the powers that make up a human person, and that is why the sociability of the worker is the kind of sociability which is likely to succeed in most cases most of the time. Considering that the working condition is the condition of most men for the greater part of their active days, this is obviously of overwhelming importance for society as well as for individuals.

A second major point in regard to the sociability of the worker may be derived from a comparison between work and art. For a number of years, I thought that work was just a particular case of art in the broadest sense of making, producing things. In this sense, art too is a transitive, external activity whose center, just as in the case of most ordinary manual labor, is in the thing made. Apart from the question of beauty, it seemed to me that work and art were barely distinguishable within the genus of productive actions. But then, not so long ago, I came to realize that even though work is like art in many respects, work as work and art as art are set apart by other than just aesthetic considerations. [15]

To put it simply, art by virtue of what makes it art is, above all, creation, and as such it proceeds exclusively from within the artist. The artist of course has to make concessions. In dealing with the pre-existent external data, he has to yield to the laws of things that are given. But this is not because of his art, for not to be pure creation and to have to compromise

---

[14] *Meta.* 982ʙ28.
[15] See Jacques Maritain, *Creative Intuition in Art and Poetry* (New York: Pantheon, 1953), Chapter ii, "Art as a Virtue of the Practical Intellect."

with some given "reality" is contrary to the nature of art. Perhaps we can use here the terms prepared in our first chapter and say that the difference between work and art is as follows: work is always an activity of legal fulfillment, art in itself is always an activity of free development. For example, I have heard that it is really quite difficult to build a vault, because this requires the mason to make heavy stones rest on thin air, as if defying the law of gravitation. We all know that the skillful placing of the stones and the pressure they exert on each other is what prevents the vaults of halls and cathedrals from collapsing unexpectedly. Nevertheless, it sometimes looks as though a "trick" were involved. Actually, there are no tricks, but on the contrary an absolute submission to the law of gravitation. That is work rather than art. The man of pure art would design his vault freely, and if it could by some magical power stay up the way he designed it, he would have no objections. The dream of every architect as artist is to be able to construct whatever he pleases to design, and to have it stay in place free from gravitation and other such things that are foreign to art. But no worker could ever build such artistic fancies. The compromise with the law of what is belongs to the very nature of work; the essence of art is to create its own reality.

We are ready now to consider how this difference between art and work affects the sociability of the artist as compared with that of the worker. First we take the artist simply as a creator; we shall consider his work (which is supposed to be a thing of beauty) later. Now clearly, the artist considered as a creator is a solitary character, and in fact most artists appear eccentric, unsocial, even antisocial. They prefer to live in the margin of society, to bewilder and scandalize, to assert themselves as individuals. We may find such behavior either ridiculous or opprobrious, and in many cases it certainly is both. Yet I see this as well in line with the essence of art understood simply as creation. In this respect, art by its very nature drives men into solitude rather than into association. As the thing he is about to bring into being must come from him alone, there is in the artist's situation absolutely nothing that calls for company. As far as I can see, this pure stuff of art as art springs from and at the same time extends the artist's own personality. However, this creative drive also inclines the artist to live in solitude and to be a socially unmanageable character. Though this may not excuse the artist as a man, it is interesting to see how his socially bad disposition is not without a foundation in the nature of art.

But what about the artist as creator of beauty? I repeat that the artist simply as creator is ruggedly individualistic. Yet as creator of beauty, he becomes another character in whom there is a specifically social element. This is so because production of beauty is essentially related to the contemplation of beauty. The beautiful being that which causes joy through contemplation, we have in this aspect of the work of art again a very obvious ground for communion. After all, why is so much money spent on the building of museums and theatres, the purchase of very expensive paintings and other objects of beauty, the beautification of cities, the construction of scenic drives, and so on? Why are all societies so interested in such things? Simply because communion in the admiration of things beautiful is an extremely important and profound way of bringing men together. In consequence of this dual nature of art, two quite opposite trends are combined in the artist: as a creator this strange fellow is an individualist, but as a creator of things beautiful he belongs rather to society. This antinomy seems to me to go a long way in explaining not only the psychology of the artist, but also the contrasting social attitudes toward the artist and toward art.

We can see now how the nature of work brings it about that the sociability of the worker stands in highly significant opposition to the social relationships of the artist. In work men must above all deal with the pre-existent data. The laws with which the workers are concerned are always to a significant extent the laws of things that already exist—like gravity —and there is nothing that the worker can do about them. A good example here is the case of agriculture, where the significance of the accidental, extraneous factors is easily grasped. Thus when the citrus crops in Florida or Texas are threatened by frost, farmers burn old tires to keep the orchards warm. This is a necessity that has nothing to do, *per se*, with the art, so to speak, of producing oranges or grapefruit; it is only when a sudden freeze threatens this crop that it becomes necessary to gather all available old tires and set them afire. The environment is thereby rendered unpleasant for several days with the worst possible smell, but, in order to keep the temperature in the orchards above the freezing point, maintaining these fires is absolutely necessary. That is definitely work. What the worker is up against are always factual necessities, which he may or may not be able to overcome, and this is where we run again into the problem of pain, difficulty, and irksomeness of work. As we have seen, these features cannot be included in the formal definition of work, for that would lead to the absurd conclusion that because he no longer experiences any irksomeness the best worker, under the best circumstances, is no longer working. Nevertheless, because work is essentially concerned with pre-existent data and with the laws that in no way depend on the things to be made, we realize that work is always something serious. The worker must forever deal with the given realities, whose resistance he often can overcome only through most strenuous effort. It is for these reasons that the worker finds himself permanently in a situation which calls for help, divisions of labor, association.

I have suggested above that the study of the grounds and

forms of sociability is an important approach to a better understanding of both the individual and society. Observing different types of sociability clarifies many things in individual psychology, in society, and even in history. Here we have seen how in contrast to the artist's lack of need for company, at least while he is in the act of creating, the worker can always use a helping hand. Moreover, in contrast to the artist's somewhat exclusive general disposition, the worker most of the time can get along with practically anybody who does his share of work. To be sure, this sociability based on work done together differs from the sociability based on joy, or love, experienced in common. But even if somewhat superficial, so to speak, the sociability of the worker is practically universal, and its value for promoting social harmony cannot be overstated. As a matter of fact, anything that frustrates it tends to contribute directly to the disruption of society. Let us illustrate this point with two contrasting examples: the first being the family constituted as a working unit, the second being slavery and alienation.

FAMILY AS A WORKING UNIT

When we read accounts of economic life in the prescientific and pretechnological age, we realize that an overwhelming amount of all work was done within the family unit. It is not without reason that our term "economy" comes from οἶκος, which means household. We have a description of this sort of economic life in the first book of the *Politics*, where Aristotle takes it for granted that what is daily and essential in the life of work is performed within the family unit. Two thousand years later, this situation had not changed much, as can be seen in Jefferson's vision of the American society.[16] True,

---

[16] For example, Jefferson held that the "cultivators of the earth" "are the most vigorous, the most independent, the most virtuous, and they are tied to

some of the farmers in early America had slaves and employed indentured servants. But within one generation after Independence that leftover from the past had practically disappeared (Negro slaves continued to work mostly on large plantations), and in its place we have the free family unit in which *people associated by matrimony and by blood are also associated at work.*

The important thing for us to grasp about this traditional family of the preindustrial age is the following. In such a unit the extremely precarious bonds of love and affection which are supposed to hold families together are constantly strengthened by the members' assocation in the daily actuality of work. Husband and wife, parents and children, can all depend here for their unity—that is, for not scattering, divorcing, or running away—on something more than just sensuous attraction, or oath of fidelity, or marital, paternal, or filial love. Working together, they all share also in the sociability of the worker. Their unity, in other words, is brought about by their common tasks, which most naturally involve a division of labor.

We have here an occasion to refer to the famous dissertation of the illustrious Durkheim. If I employ that name with a touch of irony, it is only because his school had made the

their country and wedded to its liberty and interests, by the most lasting bonds." He then described the future of America as follows: "First, we have no paupers. . . . The great mass of our population is of laborers; our rich, who can live without labor, either manual or professional, being few, and of moderate wealth. Most of the laboring classes possess property, cultivate their own land, have families, and from the demand of their labor are enabled to extract from the rich and the competent such prices as enable them to be fed abundantly, clothed above mere decency, to labor moderately and raise their families. . . . The wealthy, on the other hand, know nothing of what the Europeans call luxury. They have only somewhat more of the comforts and decencies of life than those who furnish them. Can any condition of society be more desirable than this?" The first part of this quotation is from a letter to John Jay, Paris, August 23, 1785; the second from a letter to Dr. Thomas Cooper, Monticello, September 10, 1814. See Adrienne Koch, *The Philosophy of Thomas Jefferson* (Chicago: Quadrangle, 1964), pp. 172, 174.

students of my generation quite unhappy with its rather ridiculous dogmatism. Emile Durkheim was not a great sociologist, and his stories about primitive people are not absolutely dependable. But he was a Hegelian who identified the "pure spirit" of Hegel with what he called "the collective consciousness," and his great contribution was that he found in a better understanding of that collective consciousness the promise of a new birth of morality.[17]

The stories Durkheim tells about the totemic origin of the prohibition of incest, about taboo, about Tasmanians and Australians, and so on, are not entirely reliable; but they serve the purpose of expressing a rather profound philosophical intuition. Durkheim as a philosopher sensed strongly the importance not only of the existence of the individual in society but also of the existence of society in the individual. For instance, he clearly perceived the overwhelming fact, so commonly ignored since the eighteenth century, that the moral level of each individual, with only a very few exceptions, depends heavily upon achievements of an unmistakably social character. And this is how it came about that in analyzing the division of social labor this philosophical sociologist discovered that under most circumstances it contributed toward cohesion and intimacy in social relations. In a sense, the very title of Durkheim's dissertation, *The Division of Labor in Society*, tells it all, because it is indeed in work that we find the best examples of those social divisions which cause our mutual dependence upon each other.

[17] *De la division du travail social: Étude sur l'organisation des sociétés supérieures* (Paris, 1893). In the English translation by George Simpson, *The Division of Labor in Society* (Glencoe, Ill.: Free Press, 1947), what has been usually translated as "collective consciousness" is translated as "common conscience." See also Georges Gurvitch, *Essais de sociologie* (Paris: Librairie du Recueil Sirey, 1938), pp. 115–69, especially p. 165: "La théorie de la conscience collective de Durkheim vient ici directement rejoindre la religion du 'Grand Être de l'Humanité' d'Auguste Comte et la théorie de l'Esprit absolu se réalisant dans l'Esprit objectif de Hegel."

Durkheim's thesis is rather helpful also in clarifying the meaning of the common good which obviously cannot be attained or even pursued without the cooperation, albeit in different capacities, of all the members of a given community. We can see that clearly in the example of a family constituted as a working unit. We know that, in such a family, division of labor allows its members to share in the sociability of the worker, and that the latter, by strengthening the bonds of love and friendship in the daily performance of common tasks, contributes to the stability of family life. But these observations and analyses can also be applied to the interpretation of history. The stability or lack of it of the family life have great consequences for society at large.

Let us compare the traditional situation in which most work was done in the family with the radically different conditions of work in modern times. What happened? Following a succession of industrial revolutions in the eighteenth and nineteenth centuries, and before the advent of trade unions and of social legislation, there was for an ever-increasing number of men, women, and children for a long while an enormous separation between work and family life. The consequences of this separation for both the family and society are familiar to all. When we read Marx, who is most persuasive on this subject, we become convinced that the forms of family life are necessarily affected by changes in technology and in working conditions. In fact, the *Communist Manifesto* describes the traditional marriage as having already gone to pieces in 1848, and the passage reads as if Marx did not mind. But Marx really had not given up on traditional family institutions, and he himself was very much a family man. True, it is not easy to understand why he almost let his family starve in London; while he worked all day at the British Museum writing the *Capital*, his wife and children, together with the maid, were for a time rotting in an uncomfortable, damp apartment.

He could have postponed his work on the *Capital* and taken two jobs to relieve the destitution of his family. But in principle Marx did not reject the traditional framework of family life, as did so many of his followers, including Engels who may well have been the one who started this whole tradition of cheap Marxism that we find in German Social Democracy and in French, Italian, and Spanish Socialism. Thus in the conventional social-democratic ideology, which was so important throughout Continental Europe from about the time of the death of Marx to the coming of Hitler, we find very definite ideas about family life. The leader in whatever concerned marriage was August Bebel (1840–1913), famous for his works on the emancipation of women and for his notion that the modern changes in technology and social forms had made the traditional family completely obsolete.[18] This was very loudly proclaimed by the German Social Democracy, the French Socialist Party, and all the organizations which followed their leadership.[19]

The young today might understand all this better if told again how sharp the division between the life of work and family life actually was not so many years ago. Here it is hardly possible to exaggerate. Recall the time when labor was not yet so well organized, when work days were longer, and when transportation was not so rapid. Whether or not their heart was in their work, workers spent all day every day away from their families, and when they returned home all they wanted was a chance to rest before they started out again the next morning. Interestingly enough, such life was not re-

[18] See August Bebel, *Woman and Socialism* (New York: New York Labor News Press, 1904), and *Woman Under Socialism* (New York: Socialist Literature Co., 1910).

[19] In Great Britain, it is a different story. But, then, the British Labour movement has had much less relation to Marxism, and its development must be considered within the framework of the history of the English-speaking peoples. See George Lichtheim, *A Short History of Socialism* (New York: Praeger, 1970).

stricted to the working class and the poor people exclusively. My father was an industrialist, born in 1860, and that is very much the kind of life he led, though he certainly was a family man. He could not help being gone every day before we had breakfast; he returned home for a quick lunch around noon, and then he disappeared again until 7:00 or 7:30 p.m. By then he was really tired, and so after a light meal he promptly went to bed in order to be ready to start the same kind of day the next morning. Indeed, that sort of life was quite common in that generation.

The circumstances of life and work, however, seem to be changing once again, and our philosophical analysis of past developments may help us understand what is going on now. It was not too long ago that I became aware of the emergence of a radically different situation for the masses of workers in societies leading in technological progress and social organization. Take the American working man, for he is as good an example as any; the same type may be found in some parts of Germany, in Holland, in Switzerland, in New Zealand, in Sweden, and a few other countries. In contrast to his predecessors, this new type of worker not only does not have to leave his home at dawn to get to work, but he also gets back home quite early in the afternoon and is not really exhausted. In fact, as soon as he returns, he may take up another kind of work in which his personality is more committed, and which he carries out in the framework of family dedication and family cooperation. In the second half of the twentieth century in advanced industrial countries, such working conditions and practices are becoming increasingly pervasive. Think of the millions of workers who have moved to private homes since the Second World War. Most of them enjoy the privilege of good transportation; their work in factories is generally short and light enough to leave considerable energy to be employed at home; and at home they seem to know how to do everything, including taking a television set apart and putting it back together without wrecking it or electrocuting themselves. This kind of life is not uncommon today among people who make a living working in factories, and this is a situation which almost no one foresaw a generation ago. Thus large-scale industry may be larger than ever, and the number of families working on family-size farms may be smaller than ever. But simultaneously we are also witnessing a new union of work and family life. It begins daily at 5:30 P.M. at the latest, when the wage-earner has driven home and, happy to be with his family, looks about for things to fix; he may even build a house, or at least add to the existing house as the family increases. Again, these are not isolated cases, and I do not think that it is unreasonable to expect these developments to contribute both to the strengthening of family ties and to the corresponding adjustments in other social relations.[20] After all, Marx and Durkheim derived their largely correct conclusions from observations of the same kind of developments.

SLAVERY AND ALIENATION

The importance of providing for the sociability of the worker may also be illustrated by a quick look at the institution of slavery and the alienation of the working classes in modern times. Now, when we think of work or labor in ancient times, we usually think of poor people tilling the soil from dawn to dusk and doing innumerable other chores with rather primitive tools. But we also think of slaves, serving either in private homes of the patricians or employed by the state in the construction of such famous great works as the pyramids of Egypt, the Roman aqueducts, or the Aztec monuments. Indeed,

[20] Cf. Ferdynand Zweig, *The Worker in an Affluent Society: Family Life and Industry* (New York: Free Press, 1961).

the Aztecs seem to have been as good as the Romans or the Egyptians in their ability to command huge crowds of poorly equipped workers who by virtue of their numbers, and probably also out of the fear in which they must have lived, were able to accomplish tremendous tasks. The slaves clearly were very important for the maintenance of these ancient societies. But whether they worked in private homes or for the state, these slaves were not a part of society.[21]

Thus according to the ancient political theorists, the common good is the good only of those who make up the city proper—that is, the free men, the full-fledged citizens. The slave is specifically excluded, along with the alien who might reside in the city.[22] Now, the classical theorists take a great deal of trouble to show that his exclusion from public life and his instrumental existence are advantageous to the slave. The slave by definition is incapable of acquiring the virtue of prudence; he is unable to govern himself and is therefore better off not being his own master. This is how Aristotle and his followers, with questionable success and consistency, try to vindicate the institution of slavery. They certainly do not want the slave abused or mistreated; otherwise they would not take the trouble to show that slavery is good for the slave.[23] But regardless of what else they say, there is for them no question of considering the slave a member of the civil society with a share in the common good.

What has all this to do with our discussion? Simply this: the slaves represent a particularly clear instance of workers, that is, of people who in Veblen's phrase "turn out things to human use"—who are, however, excluded from the society in which they live, work, and die. They are the original alienated.

[21] On the subject of ancient slavery in the general context of modern life and problems see Hannah Arendt, *The Human Condition*, pp. 27–29, 36n, 84–87, 119–120, and *passim*.
[22] *Politics* 7.8.
[23] *Politics* 1.6.

But alienation is a rather general concept,[24] and with the help of the preceding analysis we can perhaps make it a little more precise. What seems significant to me is that the slave is deprived not only of his human, civil rights but also of his rights as a worker. In other words, by being considered as no more than an instrument, the slave is virtually deprived also of any opportunity to exercise his sociability as a worker. I have long searched for a single expression that would put these two aspects of slavery together, but, since I have not found it, I have to use what expressions are available and adopt them to our purposes. Thus while the expression "social worker" has acquired a rather narrow, specialized meaning in our time, we may abstract from its ordinary use and signify by it the worker who is able both to practice his sociability as a worker and to enjoy his rights as a citizen. In this sense, the slave is not only not a citizen—he is an incomplete social worker. A social worker is a person whose rights both as a worker and as a citizen are fully recognized.

We may conclude this chapter by applying this analysis of men at work to a great phenomenon in modern history and society to which overwhelming social effects of yesterday, today, and tomorrow can be traced. What I have in mind is the fact that in our time uncounted millions of people have gained and are gaining access to the status of social workers in our sense. We can see this process on a large scale in the disappearance of colonialism, under which whole nations were kept in an essentially instrumental capacity for the benefit of their imperial masters. We can see it also in the so-called emancipation of the working classes in the advanced indus-

[24] See Hannah Arendt, *The Human Condition*, Chapter vi and *passim*, and Eric Fromm, *Marx's Concept of Man* (New York: Ungar, 1963). See also Robert Blanner, *Alienation and Freedom* (Chicago: University of Chicago Press, 1969); Kenneth Keniston, *The Uncommitted: Alienated Youth in American Society* (New York: Harcourt, Brace & World, 1965); Gerald Sykes, *Alienation: The Cultural Climate of Our Times* (New York: Braziller, 1964).

trial nations. People everywhere are becoming social workers. We need no more than a few such analytical tools to understand a number of problems peculiar to the present time. Marxism and socialism in general, for instance, represent to a large extent strenuous and often wayward endeavors to understand and to establish conditions for the access of all workers to the unqualified exercise of their sociability.

4

The Working Class

IN CONTINUING OUR STUDY of the relation of the working man to society, let us turn to the special case of the modern worker; here, we shall have to rely on history to a greater extent than in the preceding exposition. In other words, we are about to enter into considerations which pertain not to the nature of things but rather to the irreversible and unrenewable flow of human events. Nevertheless, this discussion offers a good opportunity for finding out what concepts produced by philosophical analysis can do for our understanding of history.

In discussing the sociability of the worker, we have developed some notions that should help us to grasp what has happened in modern times, with its rather bewildering history of work and the labor movement. Thus we may say that until about the close of the eighteenth century, the sociability of the worker was held in check by some form of servitude. At the turn of the century, and most notably in France, the situation of the working man begins to change. But for quite some time thereafter, most workers continue to be denied full membership in the civil community. The question is, Why should such a powerful kind of sociability be so consistently suppressed in history? Perhaps our approach to the historical subject of the modern working class can throw additional light on this paradoxical and much-discussed tradition.

HISTORICAL ORIGINS

First, we must go back to a period of history when the civil revolutions of the modern age may be considered to have been completed. We have of course to express ourselves in relativistic terms, for it is obvious that both the dates and the degrees of accomplishment of these revolutions vary from place to place. If we choose the time when the problem of the working class became really burning—say, 1848—that is really late, but we might make things clearer by considering the later dates. Secondly, we must ask what characterizes the social changes that had by then taken place in several countries, in Great Britain first and foremost, then in France and Germany. We shall not consider the United States except to observe that here the whole story is radically different; there is one version in the South, another in the North, and neither is like that of Europe. Moreover, in places such as Austria, Rumania, Poland, and Russia, the changes of which we speak took place much later and were probably less complete. In Italy, these changes also came much later but were perhaps not less complete than in France or Germany. In Spain and Portugal, however, all change was delayed until very much later. The atrocious civil war in Spain was in a sense a war between historical ages precisely because the political developments that had taken place in England one hundred years earlier were not yet effective there in 1936.[1]

Thus, considering England, France, and Germany—the order is roughly chronological—around the middle of the nineteenth century, we find that the principal characteristic of the changes then occurring in these countries consists in the recognition of individual, personal liberty. True, some slaves can still be found in colonial territories; but, even though tolerated, slavery becomes less and less official. Civil law is the same for all. For instance, there is no longer any difference between the several levels of society concerning inheritance. Moreover, the new principle of equal opportunity is rapidly gaining ground. I do not say that this principle was universally accepted, by any means. A German friend once told me that one reason Germany lost the First World War was that under Kaiser Wilhelm II service in the artillery was still the exclusive privilege of the sons of the nobility, whereas in the French artillery there were many commoners who also happened to be good mathematicians and who certainly excelled the German noblemen in the accuracy of bombarding enemy positions. Now, regardless of the alleged military result, higher ranks in the German artillery were in fact in 1914 still reserved mostly for the sons of the nobility. Even though not sanctioned by law, this was the factual situation in Germany. By contrast, in France the practice of offering equal opportunity to all, especially in such departments of public service as the armed forces, had been in force off and on since 1789, which is precisely why the French Revolution had

[1] Cf. Werner Sombart, *Socialism and Social Movement* (London: Dent, 1909), Appendix, "Chronological Table of the Social Movement, 1750–1907." See also William James Ghent, *Mass and Class* (New York: Macmillan, 1904); T. B. Bottmore, *Classes in Modern Society* (London: Allen & Unwin, 1965); and Roland Mousnier, *Les hiérarchies sociales de 1450 à nos jours* (Paris: Presses Universitaires de France, 1969).

stirred the whole of Europe and won sympathy among many people, even in England.

The legal suppression of servitude and the acceptance of the principles of equal opportunity were necessarily combined everywhere with greater participation of the masses in political life. Again, this was not a perfectly smooth development. Universal suffrage proclaimed by the French Revolution was soon nullified by the last constitution of the first Republic, and when Napoleon made it more universal than ever before, he almost emptied it of all real political significance. His idea was to give everybody a chance to vote, but those elected had very little initiative or actual power. Such an arrangement was also characteristic of the Second Empire. And yet, the important and irreversible change had taken place. In principle, throughout much of Europe it was established by law that any peasant or working man, any street-urchin without family, estate, or even a name or known parents, needed only some sort of identification from the Bureau of Vital Statistics to be able to share formally, even if not very effectively, in the political life of the nation.

It is in the context of these developments that, about the middle of the nineteenth century, we perceive a definite formation of the working class. In Great Britain, this class had already existed since before the end of the eighteenth century, at the latest. In France, the great industrial rush took place in the 1820s and 1830s, and the revolutionary changes it brought about included the same concentration of people in industrial cities, accompanied by destitution and misery unheard of in the past. Whether such misery was actually unprecedented is hard to tell, for there are precedents that are silent and therefore unknown. Most historians accuse capitalism of causing unprecedented destitution during those tragic decades of its early development. Yet there is some evidence that, in the precapitalistic age, people scattered throughout the extremely poor countryside were even more destitute, more starved, and worse treated.[2] But the difference is precisely that these people were scattered, whereas the industrial workers were congregated. The latter could speak with each other, could observe each other's destitution, and, most of all, could watch together the astonishing wealth that resulted from their labors. Another crucial difference was that the plight of the free industrial worker was so loudly and ably advertised. It is true that the working class or the proletariat was already in existence by the time the *Communist Manifesto* was published at the beginning of 1848. But it made a good deal of difference that it was recognized for what it was by two young men of genius, Marx and Engels, and that these intelligent social observers understood and proclaimed that something historic had taken place—namely, that a class of proletarians, the working class, had come into being.

SOCIAL ORDERS AND SOCIAL CLASSES

The meaning of the notion of social class and the distinction between the working class and the proletariat are rather complex matters, which only a few people have bothered to try to clarify. The term "proletariat" is not much used in this country, and the reason probably is that there is no proletarian class in the United States. Some years ago a friend of mine, Goetz Briefs, published in Germany a book entitled *Das gewerbliche Proletariat,* in which he set forth a deep analysis of the nature of the proletariat. I was so impressed by it that I translated it into French.[3] When, however, he later brought out in America an English version entitled *The Proletariat,*[4]

---

[2] See F. A. Hayek, ed., *Capitalism and the Historians* (Chicago: University of Chicago Press, 1954).

[3] *Le prolétariat industriel* (Paris: Desclée de Brouwer, 1936).

[4] Goetz Briefs, *The Proletariat: A Challenge to Western Civilization* (New York: McGraw-Hill, 1937).

it was a failure; I think the publisher lost money on it. Had Briefs entitled it *The Working Class*, I am certain that it would have succeeded. But that was not what the book was about, because the author had made a careful distinction between the working class and the proletariat. We shall return to this distinction presently. But first we must consider briefly the nature of the sociological entity which we call a class.

"Class" is a particularly unhappy and also mischievous word. When it is used in logic, it only brings disorder and confusion, which also happens sometimes when it is employed in the study of society. For instance, we read in countless books that ancient society was divided into three orders or classes or estates or *Stände*—namely, the clergy, the nobility, and the third estate. Even in the *Communist Manifesto*, which in addition to the history of social relations also considers carefully the history of thought about society, the meaning of the word "class" is not very specific. As everybody knows by now, the *Manifesto* begins as follows: "The history of all hitherto existing society is the history of class struggles. Freeman and slave, patrician and plebeian, lord and serf, guildmaster and journeyman, in a word, oppressor and oppressed, stood in constant opposition to one another." The very first sentence thus implies that "class" designates a sociological entity which has existed at all times, and the proletariat and the bourgeoisie, discussed later in the text, appear then merely as particular and particularly clear instances of it. This view is rather questionable. Does this mean that we should consider the proletariat in the same light as the clergy or the nobility? Or is it not true that the working class is a special type of social formation quite distinct from whatever may be called an order, or *état*, or *Stand*?

On this point, I accept fully the social and historical thinking of Goetz Briefs, who maintains that there is an essential difference between the division of society into orders and the division of society into classes, and that before the division of society into classes could become decisive, the old system of orders had to be destroyed.[5] In the *Communist Manifesto* that is not made quite so clear.

Let us, then, compare the modern division of society into classes with the division into orders under the old regime. The one involves the division between bourgeoisie and proletariat, the other that between the nobility, the clergy, and the third estate. Again, the latter division was more or less common throughout Europe prior to the French Revolution at the end of the eighteenth century. In fact, such a division has not yet completely disappeared in Great Britain, and nobody seems to be in any great hurry to abolish its remnants in the British Constitution. I do not know how costly this is, but the British seem willing to pay the price for the sake of maintaining some sort of continuity with a system which is definitely of the past. Now, according to Marx and Engels, the threefold division of the old regime was replaced by the new, simpler division that split society into the proletariat and the bourgeoisie sometime before 1848. But quite apart from their chronology, we have here the larger question of whether all these social divisions are of the same kind. And if they are not, how are they to be distinguished? How does a class differ from an order?

The best that I can do here, after having thought about it for many years (I am still not entirely satisfied), is to say that an *order* is in principle a part of an integrated society defined by a function relative to an aspect of the common good. Being "a part of society" does not distinguish an order from a class, but being "a part of an integrated society" does. An order is defined by a function relative to an aspect of the common good, and whenever there is a function to be fulfilled in

[5] Cf. Ferdinand Toennies, "Estates and Classes," *Class, Status, and Power,* edd. R. Bendix and S. M. Lipset (New York: Free Press, 1966), pp. 12–21; reprinted from "Stände und Klassen," *Handwörterbuch der Sociologie,* ed. Alfred Vierkandt (1931).

relation to the common good, this function integrates. For example, the *Republic* of Plato, with its strong, almost exclusive, emphasis on such functions, is a remarkably integrated community. By contrast, what belongs distinctly to the notion of classes—and is confirmed by empirical observation of their behavior—is that in their dynamism there is a definite tendency toward secession, which is particularly noticeable in the working class.

I do not mean to say that there were no processes of disintegration operative in the European society before the end of the eighteenth century. When speaking of the integrative functions of social orders, I have in mind mainly the ideas which presided over the constitution of this society, and which succeeded in keeping it together for impressive periods of time. In such a precarious domain as that of human affairs, this is an accomplishment that cannot be taken for granted. The idea of orders thus unifies society even when the orders fall short of perfect performance of their functions. For instance, we may say that the *clergy* is that part of society which is concerned with spiritual life. And so when the members of the clergy happen to show too much concern with things not spiritual, as in the period prior to the Reformation, we understand that this is accidental. How frequent such accidents were remains to be seen in factual investigations; accidents are frightfully frequent in human history. For monks to be interested in profits rather than in spiritual tasks, however, is perhaps roughly comparable to having extremely ambitious businessmen join labor organizations. They have no business being in labor unions, but sometimes that is where they find a way to satisfy their ambition. When we study labor organization, we view this as an accident; the same may be said for the clergy just before the Reformation.

What was the function of the order of *nobility* under the

old regime? I think it was a combination of government and military duty, in which the latter was instrumental to the former. Thus the ranks of the ancient nobility performed both the task of political government and the extremely voluminous instrumental functions of the military arm of government. This left *the third estate* for the most part with an economic function—in the modern sense of "economic," which includes not just husbandry but growing crops, transforming raw materials into finished products, transporting merchandise from one place to another, and so on. And since this third estate was supposed to be such an economic, productive order, this explains in part why they had to bear the main burden of taxation. They were the ones concerned with wealth; to have them pay taxes to keep the political-military and the spiritual parts of society operating was, in principle, a perfectly intelligible arrangement.

With due allowance for its imperfections, then, the old regime was constituted with a view toward the fulfillment by the three separate orders of certain definite functions whose objects were all clearly aspects of the common good: the good spiritual life, the good civil life, including protection against domestic disorder and against aggression from abroad, and the sufficiency of earthly goods. Of course there were conflicts, incessant and innumerable, not only between the orders but also within them. But the important thing to grasp is that there was nothing in the essence of any of these three orders that incited to secession. Let me repeat that I am not drawing a picture of an ideal peace in the old society; on the contrary, I stress the precariousness of peace in human associations. Thus allowing fully for the ever-present strife, it is nevertheless clear that so long as the old regime worked halfway as it was supposed to work—which definitely was no longer so in the most advanced countries by the end of the eighteenth century—all three of its orders were contained within the same common good. The old orders were all parts of an integrated society not the least because the idea of orders helped make it such.

Now, according to Marx and Engels, the great simplification of the capitalist era is the division of society into two classes. There is, first, the upper class, the propertied classes, the wealthy or ruling class—call it what you please. The Marxian term is *bourgeoisie*, and it seems the most appropriate, because it is from the upper or wealthy part of the old third estate that this class took shape. The other class is called by Marxists the *proletariat*. Where did it come from? Also from the third estate, but from its lower, poorer part. In fact, this new division of society into two classes is essentially a split of the third estate. This break-up occurred within about one generation after the French Revolution, and by 1848, the time we are considering, the rift is already an old thing, though consciousness of it is not yet very keen. For instance, the revolution which took place in Paris on February 24, 1848, was a democratic and social revolution, not yet a demonstration of the modern class-struggle, which was to errupt in June of the same year.[6] The people who made the revolution in February, and whose example stirred the whole of Europe, were indeed mostly workers determined to establish a social republic, a government of the people and for the people to take care of the great social issue of the destitution of the working masses. The dominating idea, however, was still the democratic ideal of "we the people," the whole people; the tendency toward secession had not yet surfaced. Even when the break came in June, and the formation of a secessionist "fourth estate" became unmistakable, the two groups (I purposely use the most indeterminate word) faced each other with no choice except to work with

[6] See John Plamenatz, *The Revolutionary Movement in France, 1815–71* (London: Longmans, Green, 1952).

each other. Neither could or wanted to crush the other completely, because without the bourgeoisie there would have been no one to pay the laborer, and without the workers there would have been no one to operate the machines. So anything like a liquidation of the bourgeoisie was out of the question, at least for the time being. And yet, the timing of the *Communist Manifesto* seems perfect. This historic proclamation was written and made public just about six months before the third estate finally split in two hostile camps and the workers appeared in the streets with a fighting revolution. The workers lost that round, but historically speaking they were on the move as a distinct social class.

This development of course did not proceed smoothly, and there were many contrary influences and historical accidents. For instance, one reason Marxism was rather slow in gaining acceptance was that many members of socialist movements were quite reluctant to give up the democratic ideal of one integrated people. This is obvious in England, and it is true of France probably more than of Germany. The rank and file of the working class were repulsed and frightened away by the call for class struggle precisely because of its secessionist implications. After the Franco-Prussian war and the experience of the Paris Commune in 1870–71, it was a common attitude among French Socialists to extol nationalism.[7] The idea that the French and the German proletarians had more in common with each other than with their respective employers was hard to accept, and it gained ground only very slowly. I do not think that it became important as a principle of social action before perhaps 1885, by which time the consciousness of class begins to be accepted by workers with increasing pride. But this development was again interfered with by war.

[7] See Daniel Ligou, *Histoire du socialisme en France, 1871–1961* (Paris: Presses Universitaires de France, 1962).

In 1914, it was believed all over the world that an armed struggle between European nations was rather unlikely —not the least because of the power and influence of socialism, which was looked upon as the movement of an international working class. By that time the Amsterdam International Organization of Workers had about 80,000 members in France and about 900,000 members in Germany.[8] The German Social Democratic Party controlled powerful unions and, being extremely well organized, was an economic and political force of the first magnitude.[9] Yet the German Socialists, with very few exceptions, voted for the war appropriations, as did the French Socialists. Afterwards, there was a great deal of recrimination and talk of betrayal, and there was some reconsideration of positions. But at the beginning of the war in 1914, the integrative principle of the national state prevailed in all countries over the secessionist tendencies of their working classes.

It must be admitted that the interpretation of the above developments varies greatly from one school of thought to another. For conservative intellectuals who tend to rely upon an ideological interpretation of history, the rise of a militant working class is the result of nothing but successful propaganda. For those at the other extreme, there is the explanation supplied by the so-called historical materialism, according to which history and the evolution of social forms are strictly determined by changes in the technological environment. And of course it has also been in fashion at one time or another to build explanations of history on climate, or geography, or heredity, or race. What all these reductionist approaches have in common is much arbitrariness, falsehood,

[8] See Julius Braunthal, *History of the International*, 2 vols. (New York: Praeger, 1967).

[9] See Guenther Roth, *The Social Democrats in Imperial Germany: A Study in Working-class Isolation and National Integration* (Totawa, N.J.: Bedminster, 1963).

and outright foolishness. But, then, interpreting history is not an easy matter, and the best we can do here is to recognize that there are always several causes at work in history.[10] To believe that the Marxian ideology could have been successful all by itself—that is, without regard to the changes in the technological environment brought about by science and industry—is clearly as naïve as to believe that modern history would have been the same without Marx. But while such gross errors may be avoided simply by relying on common sense, let us also realize that in doing so we still do not accomplish anything philosophically. Felicitous combinations of principles by the use of what is known as good sense is an approach that belongs to the practical order; for science or philosophy this is, at best, only a provisional substitute for a rational theory.

Nevertheless, in the context of our discussion, it seems rather significant that while a social *order* is not expected to secede in national emergencies, a *class* is expected to do so. In the great wars between the monarchical states of the classical age (from the sixteenth through the nineteenth centuries), the clergy, the nobility, and the middle class invariably stuck together, while the peasants simply did as they were told. Again, revolts and even civil wars may have broken out here and there, but in the case, say, of Elizabeth's England threatened by the Spanish Armada, it is really not necessary to make a point that neither the clergy, nor the nobility, nor the third estate wanted to secede. Moreover, while actual tendencies toward secession may have emerged at times on religious grounds, these religious divisions never coincided strictly with the division of society into these orders. By contrast, when we relate what happened in those fateful days of August 1914 one enormous fact stands out:

[10] Cf. Robert A. Nisbet, *Social Change and History* (New York: Oxford University Press, 1969).

the international working class did not secede as was expected. To what extent such expectation was justified is another matter. Even Lenin, who was mostly right on Russian affairs, guessed wrongly the behavior of German Socialists, and all we can say is that, obviously, he did not know Germany half as well as he knew Russia.

THE PROLETARIAT

Having clarified the meaning of *class* as opposed to *order*, let us now distinguish between the *working class* and the *proletariat*. The latter term is not customary in English-speaking countries, or at least not in the United States. I doubt if it is so rare in Great Britain, for reasons that may become clearer as we proceed. In part this is so because, to begin with, the proletariat considered as a social and historical entity is defined not primarily by the activities of its members but rather by its position in the system of exchange and distribution. Roughly speaking, the proletariat is the class of permanent and hereditary wage-earners, and that is why it is not quite identical with the working class. The working class obviously is the social entity composed of workers; furthermore, since *work* in a primary sense is manual work, it is in the main the class of those who work with their hands. It is only when these working people become permanent and hereditary wage-earners that they also become proletarians.

These features of permanence and heredity explain why the word "proletariat" is almost unknown in American society, where the opportunity for change and advancement in one's social position has been incomparably more common than elsewhere.[11] A young American who is a wage-earner today has reasonable hope of not being one twenty years

[11] Cf. Werner Sombart, *Warum gibt es in den Vereinigten Staaten keinen Socialismus?* (Tübingen: Siebeck, 1906).

hence, if he cares. Or, if he does not make it himself, the chances are that he may at least see his son become a doctor of medicine or a lawyer, and his daughter a nurse or a teacher. When poor Puerto Ricans in New York were asked "Why do you come here when you have such an unpleasant life?" they replied "We expect better things for our sons and our daughters." These people are wage-earners, perhaps even permanently. But their situation is not necessarily hereditary, and that is why there is no proletariat in America. This unique sociological entity appears only when the position of wage-earners becomes historically solidified in the economic system.

Does poverty and a low standard of living have something to do with this? Yes, but not everything, and to identify the proletariat with the poor is another of those blinding confusions which must be patiently exposed. For instance, we can hardly find a more typical example than that of the German proletariat in the few generations overlapping the First World War. These were the people who swelled the ranks of the German Socialist Party and boosted its share of the vote in Reichstag elections from about 100,000 in 1871 to just under 14,000,000 in 1919. These people were not particularly poor, and many of them were doing very well. Throughout this period, Germany was intermittently described as "America in the middle of Europe," not only because of the rate of its industrial expansion but also because of the standard of living of her working people. There were hard times, of course, especially during the inflation period following the war and later during the depression, but during the latter insane period life was not easy in the United States either. The point is that, when the system of exchange and distribution operated as it was supposed to operate, German workers enjoyed a good life, including not only good elementary education for their children but also a strong class *Bewusstsein* and organization. In contrast to an earlier experience of capitalism in England, the working-class districts in Germany had pleasant, clean homes with curtains in the windows and plenty of flowers. These symptoms of prosperity, however, do imply that the inhabitants did not save much from their wages, which might have been encouraged also by the modest system of social security established by Bismarck. And so, despite relatively high living-standards and much hygiene—but practically no savings—whoever was a wage-earner was quite likely to remain a wage-earner and to transmit this condition to his descendants.

The decisive aspect here seems to be the relation between purchasing power and actual expenses which are determined, as we all know so well, not exclusively by biological needs, but by an extremely complex and changing combination of biological needs and needs of a social character. (In medieval theology, these needs were distinguished as *necessarium vitae* and *necessarium status*.) To wear a necktie is not required for biological survival, but in a certain social condition it is indispensable to own a necktie, or even a tuxedo. Another telling example of strange combinations of what is biologically and what is sociologically necessary is the following. Not so long ago, expensive pills and extremely expensive medical treatment were considered luxuries, accessible only to the privileged part of society; in our time, however, expensive medical treatment is beginning to be generally considered to belong to those vital necessities on which one cannot compromise.

We see, then, that a solid proletarian condition may exist in the midst of relative plenty. But if the income of the workers reaches a certain level allowing for a real possibility of saving, and if there are no other social restrictions, then the wage-earner's condition is no longer permanent and hereditary. Such seems to have been the state of affairs in America, and the reason that the word "proletariat" is so little used here. An abundance of land, ready credit, and high wages resulting in part at least from the shortage of labor, have made the position of the wage-earner in the United States non-permanent and non-hereditary.

Nevertheless, American experience cannot be accepted as evidence that an economy largely free from public institutional control does not necessarily lead to the division of society into classes and an eventual formation of the proletariat. This is so because the central institution of a *laissez-faire* system is the free market where labor is just another item of merchandise, the sale and the price of which are determined by the so-called law of supply and demand. Thus when there is a shortage of labor, wages will be high; but when labor is plentiful—or jobs become scarce—wages go down; and if this situation recurs regularly the formation of the proletariat is inevitable. Of course, where there are pensions for old age, unemployment and health insurance, state control of prices or rates, minimum-wage laws, and the like, combined with strong labor-union organization, the law of supply and demand becomes much less important, and the exact position of the working man in the system of distribution and exchange is no longer so sharply defined. But, then, as everyone realizes, that is no longer a free-market system.

Throughout much of history, workers have been alienated from society and their sociability held in check through a variety of forms and degrees of servitude. But in modern times we have the paradox of men who are free in a civil and political sense, who are in law equal to their fellow countrymen, but who have no estate. As Goetz Briefs points out very clearly—what has seldom been dared—the crucial fact of modern society is the coexistence of freedom and of privation.[12] Modern society seems to have discovered something that all previous ages have denied—namely, that it is possible, at least for a time, to give men the burden of freedom without letting them have either property or a social function to help them carry that burden. The proletariat is the result of this unique discovery. Again, the proletarians are not just people who engage in a certain kind of activity—namely, manual work—nor are the proletarians just the poor people. The proletarians as a social class are defined by their position in the system of exchange and distribution known as the free market. Because labor in this system is a commodity bought and sold in the market, the working man becomes a sort of unit of exchange, and the community of the working people, as if by an enormous accident, becomes a distinct social class which, deprived of a functional share in the common good, develops a strong tendency toward secession.

Let us make it clear that, although poverty is not necessarily implied in the proletarian condition, subjection is. True, we are all subject to some sort of authority most of the time, and we find that entirely normal. But there is something about the subjection of the proletariat which has been particularly resented, especially in the earlier phases of the labor movement. This peculiarity of the proletarian condition may be best explained by pointing out that every community normally tends to achieve autonomy. This is a sort of law: wherever there is a normal community, there is also a tendency toward autonomy. We may observe this inclination even among children, not so much in their disobedience and rebellion against adult authority as in their mutual relations, which even among very young children may be quite elaborate, allowing us the privilege of witnessing the social genius of mankind at work. The degree of autonomy, however, that

[12] *The Proletariat*, pp. 14ff; 247ff.

is in fact achievable by different communities varies greatly, and we use the expression "maturity" to designate the condition for a more complete and normal degree of autonomy. This is a relationship which is in great need of clarification, but let it suffice here to say that, no matter how high the degree of genuine autonomy, autonomy does not necessarily require resistance to authority.[13] For instance, though there might be some extreme Platonists among us who would not mind seeing the family disappear through a functional integration of state and society, most of us remain in favor of some autonomy for the family community. Yet when we defend this autonomy against the Platonists, we do not mean to say that the family does not have to obey any state laws, any more than we mean that no one has to take orders within the family community itself. What we mean is that the business which is clearly family business should normally be settled by processes of family self-government.

By analogy, when we speak of the subjection of the proletariat (regardless of whether or not there is poverty), we assume that the proletariat is a community with some business as well as a consciousness of its own. Now, this consciousness of the working class is rather an old affair. Marx and Engels contributed a great deal to it, but had it not already existed, at least in an incipient state, they could not have written the *Communist Manifesto*. What is important to realize is that this consciousness of the working class is not merely an awareness of community; it also includes the awareness that by reason of its place in the market system of exchange and distribution this class has no autonomy, that it has no power of self-government. That this is in fact so becomes quite clear when we observe how the situation of the working class has been radically transformed by measures

---

[13] See Yves Simon, *General Theory of Authority*, especially Chapter IV, "The Communication of Excellence."

and institutions, above all the labor unions, which enhance the workers' autonomy. The recognition of the labor unions by law appears here to have been the decisive development. Today, public powers sanction, albeit somewhat reluctantly, even such questionable practices as the closed shop and the union shop. But even though these practices may be considered somewhat arrogant, they are nevertheless plainly recognizable as actions of a community asserting its autonomy. Moreover, the tendency of social legislation in the last thirty to thirty-five years has been to provide, in varying degrees, for some sort of workers' representation on the job. In many countries, delegates are now elected among workers to share in the management of enterprises.[14] All these trends are expressions and embodiments of the autonomy of the working class, and as they increase, the proletarian features of the workers' situation necessarily become less marked.

But besides poverty, which is not essential, and subjection, or lack of autonomy, which is essential to its condition, there is another feature which characterizes the typical proletariat. This third characteristic of the proletariat is the denial of social consideration, and, for an understanding of modern history it may indeed be the most important of all. Such a denial has always been among the most powerful causes of social restlessness and revolutions. But in the case of the proletariat, it assumes a special significance for two reasons. One is that the proletariat is composed of people who under law are free and even equal to the owners of property. The other is that this denial of social consideration takes place in the face of glorification of work, which is something found seldom in history before modern times. We have dealt with the first of these two reasons in the above discussion of the historical

[14] See Adolf I. Sturmthal, *Workers Councils*, Wertheim Publications in Industrial Relations (Cambridge: Harvard University Press, 1964), for a recent study of these developments in France, Germany, Poland, and Yugoslavia.

origins of the working class; the second deserves further treatment.

The exaltation of work in modern times was mentioned in the opening pages of this book to clear the ground for an objective approach to a definition of work. Here we have an opportunity to test the ability of our approach to clarify not only the nature of things social but also history. The question is, Why is the denial of social consideration unacceptable to working people in modern times? Part of the answer is that the working class has been winning its political battles. But that is not all. I think that work too has come into its own, so to speak—namely, that there has been progress in the understanding of the nature of work as a human and social activity. Let us see how much the ideology of the working class has contributed to this understanding.

THE IDEOLOGY OF THE WORKING CLASS

I call ideology a system of views relative to subjects of philosophic import, such as work, but which are held: 1.) in a particular society, 2.) at a given period in its evolution, and 3.) in answer to definite needs.[15] In other words, an ideology involves interpretation of truth which is sociological, evolutionistic, and pragmatic. There are, of course, people who say that all philosophy, in the last analysis, is ideology. But though this has been quite a popular view in modern times—witness Pragmatism and the sociology of knowledge —we do not have to accept it as the last word.

Clearly, no genius is required to show that there are many and rather obvious cases in which a so-called philosophy is little more than an expression of certain ideas accepted in a particular society because of their agreement with the tendencies of that society at a given time in history. Any of us can

[15] See Yves R. Simon, *The Tradition of Natural Law*, ed. Vukan Kuic (New York: Fordham University Press, 1965), pp. 16–27.

take brilliantly successful philosophical ideas and show how wonderfully they agree with significant tendencies of the community in which they are so well received. What is much more difficult, however, is to remove carefully all such pragmatic components and to get down to the philosophic core of an ideology, at least where, as I think happens in most instances, there is such a core. Indeed, every once in a while we even find a philosophical system with no admixture of ideological components to speak of. Take Spinoza (1632–1677), for instance. Practically none of his ideas is traceable to the evolution of the merchant middle class which was asserting itself in Holland in his time. Thus "Spinozism" is a very clear and significant case of a philosophy (whether it is a good philosophy or not is not the issue) that is remarkably independent of the factors which make up an ideology. By contrast, in the case of John Locke (1632–1704) we find that ideological components are quite voluminous in his philosophy. Here we have a whole philosophical system, including some sort of logic, psychology, metaphysics, an interpretation of religion, and, above all, a theory of government, none of which is free of notions fitting rather nicely the preferences of the Anglo-Saxon, English-speaking society of his time. Another case of a philosophy relatively free of ideology is that of Aristotle. But in regard to subjects such as slavery and work, he may not have completely escaped the influence of the ideas predominant in the society in which he lived. Cartesianism represents still another philosophy in which the pressure of ideology seems negligible. But in the works of Herbert Spencer (1820–1903), we have again a good example of a philosophy which is principally, if not entirely, reducible to an ideology. His publisher, if not the philosopher himself, certainly realized that Spencer's views represented the synthesis demanded by the industrial age, especially in English-speaking society.

Many more examples could be cited, but these few suffice to show that when they are present the ideological components of a philosophic system are usually easy to recognize. What is hard but much more worthwhile is to go after the philosophic core of an ideology—that is, after the truth that is at variance with ideology precisely because it is independent of society, because it is independent of history, and, above all, because it is independent of human needs and aspirations.

Now, it seems to me that among the main tenets of the ideology of the working class the following three stand out. The first is the principle of social utility of work; the second is a feeling of earnestness; and the third is the desire to participate in the glamor of modern science. That all these notions fit nicely the needs and the aspirations of the working people is fairly obvious. But they are also related to certain metaphysical, socio-ethical, and sociological characteristics of work which we have considered in the theoretical part of our discussion. Let us see whether this coincidence can help us throw additional light on several aspects of the history of the labor movement, of socialism, and of modern times.

Concerning the principle of social utility of work, it will be recalled that we have made it an essential part of our theoretical definition of work, over and above common honesty. Thus burglars do not work; financial speculators do not work; contemplatives do not work. Why? Because none of them in doing what they do is rendering any service to society. Of course, being useful is also a metaphysical characteristic of work: work is never a terminal activity but always leads to something else. Utility, therefore, besides being a tenet of the ideology of the working class has a relation to the philosophic understanding of work as a human activity. But in the proletarian ideology this principle is qualified in two ways whch are crucial for the understanding of modern history.

First, the proletarian notion of social utility is colored by an interpretation obviously received from the bourgeoisie. It is very much like that articulated by the economists in the ideology of the successful industrial and merchant middle class, long before the development of the working-class consciousness. In this view, social utility is something which is not to be transcended, a sort of an ultimate standard. For me, this is a crucial point. A person may be dedicated with all his heart to works socially useful, and most of the time there is hardly anything more worthwhile for any one of us to do. But to know that the socially useful may some day be transcended by something that is not useful but terminal, something which is beyond utility, makes an all-important difference. In our theoretical analysis of work, we have set the terminal character of contemplation in sharp opposition to the mere usefulness of work; in the ideology of the worker that is out of the question. The notion of social utility received by the working class from the bourgeois social thinkers refers to a utility that is not accompanied by any endeavor to transcend it. It is, in other words, the utility of a society in which there is no room for contemplation, where contemplatives are considered idlers.

Secondly, the notion of social utility in the proletarian ideology identifies social utility with the transformation of physical nature for the satisfaction of man's needs. As we have seen, this idea too emerges at the end of the eighteenth century, at the very latest, and it includes the belief that all activities of a social, civic, or political character tend to represent exploitation of man by man. This was one of the main tenets of Saint-Simonism, and it is easy to see how it produced at first an anarchistic theory of society. If the purpose of human activity is to control physical nature, and if anything which is not that represents exploitation of man by man, then what we ought to have is a society which follows the engineers in the transformation of nature but remains in all other respects free from any authority. Such indeed is the common anarchism of the labor movement, which the Marxists had to incorporate into their ideology whether they liked it or not. It was Marx's friend (by no means his equal) Frederick Engels, who uttered the famous prophecy that, when the exploitation of the majority by the few has come to an end, *"der Staat wird absterben"*—the state will die out. I do not know who coined it, but there is another wonderful English rendition: "the withering away of the state." The state will not be violently abolished, it will disappear for lack of an object. We find this notion in the entire working-class movement, including, as already mentioned, the American Federation of Labor. Its founder Gompers was by no means a man of violent action; yet he too was a kind of anarchist who thought that, when the problems of justice in economic relations had been solved by proper economic and labor organization, then the state would disappear. What seems particularly significant is that today we do not hear much discussion of this idea anywhere; it is gone. During the Second World War, I expected that for a while after the downfall of the dictatorships there would be a new wave of anarchism. I was wrong. It did not come, and I do not see it anywhere; the specific idea of the withering away of the state now belongs to the ideology of another age.

Concerning the feeling of earnestness in the ideology of the working class, it will be recalled that necessity and seriousness have been mentioned repeatedly among the socio-ethical elements of our theoretical definition of work. But here let us also recognize that both the feeling of social utility and the feeling of earnestness set the ideology of the working class in strong opposition to the concept of culture which has been predominant in the last few centuries. As already mentioned, in the seventeenth century, at the latest, there appeared a cultural ideal best conveyed by the French name for the type of person who embodied it—*honnête homme*. Blaise Pascal (1623–1662), who had something to do with promoting this ideal, wrote in his *Pensées*: "We should be able to say of a man not that he is a mathematician, a preacher, or eloquent, but that he is a gentleman. This universal quality alone pleases me." [16] Just before the French Revolution, this standard was perhaps no longer universally admired, but the typical culture-bearer throughout the nineteenth century still fits Voltaire's description in *Le mondain*: "*J'aime le luxe, et même la mollesse, Tous les plaisirs, les arts de toute espèce, la propreté, le goût, les ornements, Tout honnête homme a de tels sentiments.*" [17]

A life of leisure and pleasure was thus until recently not only a badge of culture; it was the very expression of culture. Think, for instance, of the life of the aristocracy and the rich bourgeoisie, say, in old Vienna, which was the loveliest of all frivolous cities except, perhaps, Paris. We have to take one of these two rather than, say, London or Berlin. Whenever Berlin tried to imitate Paris or Vienna, it became quite pitiful, and London did not try to imitate them. Even to this day, Vienna and Paris appear to have remained the two main centers of leisure adorned by culture, and that may well be one of the reasons that we all like to go there whenever we have the opportunity.

An opposite notion of culture, however, a notion of culture based on work in the broadest sense, appears no longer completely absurd today. One of the reasons for this change in outlook is that in the movement of the working class we

[16] Fragment 35 (Modern Library edition, p. 14).
[17] *Selections from Voltaire*, ed. George R. Havens (New York: Holt, Rinehart & Winston, 1949), p. 101.

find an historic and history-making striving toward a culture which is to be something serious, something marked by the same earnestness that presides over the life of work. I urge this point especially for the interpretation of the cultural life in this country.[18] American society is dominated, at least in its more valuable segments, by the psychology of the worker —that is, by a fundamental disposition characteristic of people who do something socially useful and who are dedicated to serious life. I suppose that this is what some intellectuals attribute to Puritanism, which is a perfect example of the abuse of such key ideas in the explanation of history. Indeed, when some literary gentleman begins to explain the essence of American society by reference to Puritanism, the chances are that he will be talking nonsense. What he probably has in mind is the feeling of earnestness that prevails in this society where, in contrast to the aspirations and habits of the European bourgeoisie, everybody works, housewife and children included.

Finally, we come to the most interesting and difficult subject—namely, the relation between the ideology of the working class and modern science. Here again we find a connection with a philosophical problem already touched upon —namely, the question whether work is a rationally directed activity. That the position of modern workers on that issue should be the opposite of that apparently taken by Aristotle or Plato comes as no surprise, for obvious ideological reasons. But what is much more interesting is the sense in which the proposition that work is a rationally directed activity finds independent and overwhelming support in the development of modern science. Let us recall that, as the manual worker is the prototype of worker, work means primarily the transformation of physical nature for the purposes of man. But

---

[18] See the Foreword to *La Civilisation Américaine,* ed. and trans. Yves R. Simon (Paris: Desclée de Brouwer, 1950), pp. 7–20.

through the development of what I call the demiurgical tendency—that is, the technological orientation of natural sciences—this is now also the primary meaning of Science. For most people, Science means precisely the power of transforming that physical nature which the knowledge of the laws of nature places in man's hands. Moreover, today much of the work that has to be done in order that society may survive is in fact done scientifically—that is, rationally—rather than empirically. A "mechanic" today is hardly the automaton Aristotle imagined him to be, and the word carries quite a different connotation than it did even as late as the founding of the United States, when some of the framers of the American Constitution doubted that the "mechanics" in the towns were fully qualified for citizenship. Or, to refer to another of our earlier examples, not much liquor, relatively speaking, is produced today by chewing corn and spitting it into a barrel. Is it any wonder, then, that both work and the worker are judged differently in modern times than in the past?

Indeed, throughout the history of the working class, there persists the feeling that its movement coincides with the movement of intelligence in modern society, characterized especially by the technical power of science. Since we have here a group which is composed of people who deal directly with physical nature, we can easily understand why scientism is so prominent in the ideological expressions of the working class. In one way or another, all socialist schools of thought—including those derived from the teachings of Saint-Simon and Comte as well as Marx—have their roots in that great expression of scientific enthusiasm in the eighteenth century, the great French *Encyclopédie*. But let us also realize that this way of thinking, which may well be called pragmatism, represents the ideology not of the working class only but basically of the modern society as a whole. Indeed, long before workers themselves first claimed to be bearers not only of social but of intellectual progress as well, the advance of modern science had turned work into something pertaining to the life of knowledge.

To sum up: The ideology of the working class is characterized first of all by an almost religious dedication to social utility. Secondly, it is characterized by a feeling of earnestness, which goes against the grain of the ideal of Culture that has prevailed in Europe in modern times. Thirdly, the ideology of the working class is characterized by a feeling of kinship with Science, which includes a desire to be recognized as an agent in the transformation not only of physical nature but also of society. None of these notions, however, belongs exclusively to the working class, and it can truly be said that they were all bourgeois ideas and ideals before they became appropriated by the working-class ideology.

The rise of the working class was greatly facilitated by the belief that the bourgeoisie—we are speaking primarily of Europe—had become parasitical and could no longer lead mankind toward the promised future. Even in the *Communist Manifesto* the bourgeoisie is condemned only after its achievements had been praised as greater than those of all previous ages. But according to the working-class ideology, bourgeois practice had given the lie to its ideals of serious dedication to work and to the pursuit of knowledge for the sake of asserting man's power over nature. Having become rich, the bourgeoisie turned to imitating the aristocracy by adopting a way of life symbolized by the ideal of a leisurely and slightly frivolous culture. We do not have to decide here which side has the truth to recognize that this argument is the gist of the ideological battles that are still going on. But if we are to attempt to clarify this issue, it is clear that we should need to have some idea about what may well be at the heart of the human and social problem of the future— namely, the relationship between work and wealth. The following chapter is devoted to that subject.

5

Work and Wealth

As WE HAVE SEEN, the modern worker has often enough been also a proletarian, and the proletarians as a class are characterized by a tendency toward secession. These people do not feel that they are an integral part of society; they do not feel, for instance, that the police are their police but rather the police of someone else. Why do they feel that way? Because they are mostly poor, because they are denied all social consideration, and because, as a class, they lack autonomy. As we have just seen, all these things have been the primary targets of the various socialist and labor movements in the past century or so. But these matters deserve as much theoretical as historical treatment, and from a theoretical point of view two great subjects seem to be involved: the first is the relation of work to wealth, the second the relation of work to culture. Let us in this chapter consider the relation of work to wealth, both in general and in regard to current

116

social problems; and let us treat the relation of work to culture in the same manner in our last chapter.

By way of introduction to the first of these topics, we may ask this simple but decisive question: Is work necessarily relative to some sort of wealth either to be produced or to be acquired? This question is more or less of the same kind as the one raised about the irksomeness of work at the very beginning of our discussion. Does it belong in the formal definition of work? My answer is again "No." The reason for the negative answer is that, even though I recognize that in most cases there is some connection between work and wealth, if we included the relation to wealth in the formal definition of work, we would be at a loss to explain a number of activities which obviously are work though they are in no way related to wealth. Take, for instance, a physician treating a patient without fee. Does that mean that he is not working? Of course not; he is working hard. And yet there is no wealth produced or acquired here. The surgeon gets nothing for his services, and the patient is restored to health, which is better than any kind of wealth. Health, being internal to man, is an autonomous good, something desirable for itself; wealth, being external to man, is a mere utility, forever a means to something else.[1] Because work, which too is a means, can sometimes be a means to an autonomous good, we understand that its relation to wealth is not essential. But in the overwhelming majority of cases, men work either to produce or to acquire some sort of wealth, and when things are considered in relation to psychological and social realities what happens in the overwhelming majority of cases is decisive.

Accordingly, we can state that the objective and primary function of labor is the production of wealth. In order to proceed, however, we have to have as clear a definition of

[1] See Aristotle, *Ethics* 1.3. 1096B6. *Politics* 1.8 1246B30; Thomas Aquinas, *Summa Theologica* Ia, q. 5, a. 6.

"wealth" as possible. Now, in economic theory, the term "wealth" designates any physical reality exterior to man, the use of which is necessary or favorable to the support and expansion of human life. Notice that by saying *physical reality* we remove the analogical extension of the notion of wealth to spiritual or ethical values, while by saying *exterior to man* we also remove from the notion of wealth the physical goods inherent in human persons, such as health or beauty. In other words, wealth always has the character of a merely useful good, or a mere means.[2] Consider, for instance, various kinds of real wealth: houses, clothes, food, vehicles, scientific instruments. Anyone can easily see that the end is not in wealth but always in man. (Money, which is a means for acquiring real wealth, besides being a practical measure of wealth, is a means for a means.) Strictly speaking, then, the concrete ultimate end of work lies in the human use of wealth rather than in the wealth itself. For the sake of brevity, however, we can say that wealth is the end intended by the worker, provided that in our understanding of wealth we include wealth itself, which is but a means, and the human use of it, which is at the same time the end both of wealth and of work.

SERVICE AND PROFIT OF WORK

Work and wealth are related in several ways which are not easily grasped all at once, and we shall therefore proceed gradually by simple examples. For instance, a family living on and operating a small farm, which was used in Chapter 3 as an example of a closely knit, integrated working-unit, embodies an important type of relationship of work to wealth.

[2] See Yves Simon, "Work and Wealth," *The Review of Politics*, 2, No. 2 (April 1940), 197–217. Cf. J. A. Hobson, *Work and Wealth: A Human Valuation* (New York: Macmillan, 1922).

Though we sometimes hear stories of corn farmers or even hog farmers who buy frozen pork chops at the supermarket, there are still left in the world a number of small farms where not much cash is needed because cows are kept to produce milk, pigs to produce pork chops, hens to produce eggs, and so on. For the people on these farms, the economically significant factor is the production of things to be consumed or used by themselves. For us, the significant factor in their example is the unity of what I shall call service and profit of work, to be explained presently.

Completely self-sufficient households, however, have probably always been exceptional, and they would indeed be very difficult to find today. Therefore, let our next example be that of a farming family who produce things not exclusively for domestic use but also for sale in the market. The latter does not have to be an extensive operation for us to see immediately that we have here a radically different relation of work to wealth, in which the unity of service and profit is gone, and a new factor—that of exchange—has been introduced. Trying to keep it simple, let us suppose that this family keeps hens to produce eggs for the market, where they are sold for cash or used in barter. In either case, there is the all-important question of exchange: How much money are, say, two dozen eggs worth? How many eggs equal a pair of shoes? In an actual market place, this might not be much of a problem, as the eggs would be sold at the going price. But in economic theory, and in social theory, the matter is by no means simple, as can plainly be seen in the large number of price theories and the huge amount of social criticism of the market system. Everyone understands that an exchange is just and proper insofar as the things exchanged are equal;[3] but determining the value of things to be exchanged is never easy. In reference to our example, what about the condition

[3] *Summa Theologica* IIa IIae, q. 61, a. 2.

of the eggs? Clearly, this too enters the problem of exchange, and I have a true story to illustrate how complex it can get. Some time ago, I met a gentleman who told me that his family's fortune was started when his father went around peddling frozen eggs as if they had been laid that very day. Now the biological and nutritional properties of eggs properly frozen at the right time might be very much like those of fresh eggs, and so only a little lie was here employed. Yet, if we receive for frozen eggs the same price as we would get for fresh eggs and make a fortune, this clearly has economic and social consequences which are not so easily explained or calculated. We need but a few such examples in order to understand that production for exchange represents a distinct type of the relation of work to wealth, the decisive characteristic of which is that here work is not directly related to the use of wealth.

Let us try to state the general conditions of such situations as precisely as possible. What happens in production for exchange is that the producer, be he a worker or an entrepreneur, intends at the same time to satisfy the customers and to make money, and the primary finality of work is thereby divided into what I call *service* and *profit*. The sense in which I use these terms is as follows. Inasmuch as it is destined for human use, wealth produced by work constitutes the service of work. But the workman has to secure his own maintenance by his work, which, therefore, can only very rarely be a gratuitous gift. Accordingly, either the worker himself is the beneficiary of his service, the user of the wealth he produces, or he exchanges the service rendered to another for a theoretically equivalent amount of wealth—which is what I here call profit. Whenever there is production not directly for use but for exchange, service and profit of work are separated, and, depending upon the distance between them, the life and the meaning of work vary deeply from one situation to another.

When this distance is short, as in the case of a handicrafts-man in a small town who keeps up daily relations of co-citizenship and neighborhood friendship with the benefi-ciaries of his services, the subordination of profit to service is comparatively easy both to understand and to achieve. (This is the proper relationship, because the real wealth produced by work is above all destined to serve; profit is but a counter-part of service, a result annexed to the essential product of labor activity.) The handicraftsman in a small town need not be a moral hero to understand that his profit is legitimate only insofar as it is a compensation for honest services.

But as the distance between service and profit increases, the relation between work and wealth tends to be confused. In modern times, this has been the prevailing state of affairs. For instance, in *The Theory of Business Enterprise*, noting that it is the sale which is the last step and the end of a businessman's endeavor, Veblen writes:

> The vital point of production with him is the rendibility of the output, its controvertibility into money values, not its service-ability for the needs of mankind. A modicum of serviceability, for some purpose or other, the output must have if it is to be sale-able. But it does not follow that the highest serviceability gives the largest gains to the business man in terms of money, nor does it follow that the output need in all cases have other than a ficti-tious serviceability. . . .[4]

This is not an unfamiliar complaint, as businessmen through-out history have never enjoyed an unblemished reputation. But to grasp its significance here, this example should be

[4] P. 50 (New York: Scribners, 1904). See also Horace Taylor, *Making Goods and Making Money* (New York: Macmillan, 1928).

complemented by recalling also Lafargue's cynical remark about the wage-earners who would not object at all to a system which would permit them to earn their wages without working.[5] When there is separation of service and profit, the psychology of the worker tends to resemble that of the businessman, because under modern conditions he seems to have almost no choice but to work for profit rather than for service of work.

Again, whenever there is work to produce wealth for exchange rather than for use, there is separation of service and profit of work, resulting in confusion about the concrete ends of work as well as of wealth. There is no metaphysical necessity in any of this, but as a psychological and social reality this uncertainty about the end of work and wealth has the character of a determinate tendency, which seems to have been brought about mostly by modern techniques of production and distribution. Among the consequences of this state of affairs, I wish to draw attention especially to these two typical situations: one is the lack of quantitative proportion between service and profit of work, the other is represented by the proliferation of illusory services.

To illustrate the first situation, let me again recall a true story. Not so long ago, when a doctor paid a visit at the home of a patient and charged anything from five to ten dollars, this was considered a reasonable reward for a real service. But there is the famous case of a certain doctor who once examined a promising young lawyer and politician by the name of Franklin D. Roosevelt. The doctor found the patient in bed, examined him, and told him that he had a cold; then, after prescribing some aspirin and rest, the doctor left. When, however, a few days later the ailment turned out

[5] Paul Lafargue wrote *The Evolution of Property from Savagery to Civilization* (New York: Scribners, 1894).

to be poliomyelitis, this doctor sent in a bill, not for $10.00, but for $600.00—a rather striking example of the lack of quantitative proportion between the service rendered and its price.

Concerning the second typical consequence of the separation of service and profit of work—namely, the proliferation of illusory services—we must note first of all that this very notion of an illusory service is not welcome, to say the least, in certain schools of economic thinking. Instead of analyzing such problems as the relation of work and wealth, what most economists seem to like to do is to be very empirical and merely to observe the goings-on in the market. This focal point of the economists' attention is a peculiar place where all kinds of desires are expressed and where people pretend that they can satisfy those desires. So the parties bargain until they reach an agreement on the price, and that is all there is to it. The notion of an illusory service, therefore, has no place in the theory of the market economy.

Nevertheless, what is denied in theory is plainly recognized in practice, as for example in the control of the distribution of drugs harmful to human health. But a thing does not have to be actually harmful in itself in order to be an illusory service. For instance, in our society whole teams of salesmen are dedicated to importuning people until they break down and buy huge cars which they really do not need. For this the dealers collect a handsome profit, as do those who manufacture the car, the auto workers not excluded; but the customer most of the time gets something which is entirely out of proportion, on the one hand, to the financial burden assumed with this purchase, and, on the other, to his actual needs. As far as the customer is concerned, the car is too powerful, too luxurious, and too expensive—a good example indeed of an illusory service. Certain economists, of course, would say that that is what the customer wants, and they see nothing wrong with it.[6] But their saying so does not make the notion of illusory service irrelevant, nor does it prevent proliferation of illusory services from having economic and social consequences, some of which are objectionable from a moral standpoint, but some of which, as we shall see, may in addition lead objectively to economic and social disaster.

Clearly, what we are facing here is a huge field of philosophic, moral, economic, and social investigation, in which a great deal of research has yet to be done. The problem to which I am calling attention is this. No economic theory can do without a clear concept of wealth; but no concept of wealth is, in the last analysis, intelligible without some reference to use or service, which in turn requires an understanding of human nature and of what is good for man. My job as a philosopher is to raise doubts about the obviousness of the economists' empiricism. To deny that there is such a thing as an illusory service means to assert that any and every desire is an expression of genuine need, which is something no one really believes, despite all professions to the contrary. From their personal experiences, the economists like everyone else know well that not every desire is an expression of genuine need. In fact, there are very few economists who insist, without any qualifications, that there is absolutely no difference, from a strictly economic point of view, between what may be called ordinary consumption and what Veblen has called "conspicuous consumption." But if this distinction is admitted, then a critical theoretical as well as historical study of the relation of work and wealth and of the notion of real wealth cannot be completely excluded from economic inquiry.

[6] Among the economists who have criticized this notion of "consumer sovereignty" is John Kenneth Galbraith, who recently exposed it as a hoax. See his *The New Industrial State* (Boston: Houghton Mifflin, 1969), especially Chapter XIX, "The Revised Sequence."

In order to avoid misunderstanding, let us recognize that the concrete notion of real wealth varies considerably according to time, place, social environment, and customs. The objective determination of real wealth, therefore, presupposes in addition to the right philosophy of man a detailed acquaintance with historical periods and with the peculiarities of different societies. But even then the question whether something constitutes true wealth for a particular society at a given historical moment cannot always be answered with complete certainty. For instance, what about the discrepancy between desire and need, the so-called "conspicuous consumption"? Does it occur more often in modern, economically highly developed societies, or in the older and less technically developed societies? One reason which suggests that it may be more widespread in our society is that where there are large markets and advanced means of mass communication, there is also a great deal of advertising, which is likely to amplify factual desires far beyond genuine needs. And yet, since we are so much better informed about what is going on in our own time, it is by no means absolutely certain that, for some other reason (rather than large markets and persistent advertising), the situation might not have been just as bad centuries ago. Even to begin to speculate about it, however, one needs to have some conception of real wealth, and that is all that needs to be understood here for the moment.

What bears repeating is that this whole problem of the relation between work and wealth depends on recognizing and admitting something that many economists want to leave out of the picture altogether—namely, the possibility of a discrepancy between human desire and genuine human need. For many economists, the beginning and the end of their discipline is in the market place where people with definite desires bargain with people who claim that they can satisfy those desires. In my view, this is an arbitrary limitation of the scope of the science of economics, and the boast that this approach is free from value judgments is nothing but a myth. Modern economics has been the main source of reinforcement in all social sciences for the postulate which Max Weber called *Wertfreiheit*—best translated as ethical neutrality, and, were this postulate valid, what we are speaking of here would be irrelevant, at least from the point of view of economists. But there is no obvious necessity to accept the postulate of ethical neutrality in any science dealing with society, and perhaps least of all in economics.[7] When we consider the absurdity of a compensation for service which is not genuine but illusory; when we notice that this is not a rare accident in our economic life (which it might have been five hundred years ago); when we try to calculate the amount of wealth leaking out of society through payments for such ungenuine services—when we add all these things together, we can never be convinced that the concept of genuine service of work, as distinguished from mere satisfaction of just any desire, is not relevant from the point of view of a science that deals specifically with wealth.

WORK AS A COMMODITY

That service to society is an essential element in the notion of work was established in general terms in Chapter 2. Here we shall deal with the special case of illusory services and their possible economic and social causes and consequences. As has just been suggested, some of these illusory services are clearly objectionable from an ethical point of view, and are even checked by law—for instance, the distribution of drugs harmful to human health. Moreover, illusory services cannot but have a detrimental effect on both the psychology and the

[7] See Yves Simon, "From the Science of Nature to the Science of Society," *The New Scholasticism*, 27, No. 3 (July 1953), 280–304.

sociability of the worker, and must, therefore, be suspected of being a contributing source of frustration and alienation of the working class. But in the final analysis, illusory services are objectionable also from a formal economic standpoint because of the possibility that by crippling the system of distribution they may annul the genuine service of work.

With the great economic depression of the 1930s, the twentieth century really became absurd. For instance, in a kind of sick joke often told at the time, a farmer who made money raising and selling pigs is deeply disappointed to find out that another farmer had made much more money by butchering some of his pigs and keeping them off the market. This was the time when in Brazil coffee was used to stoke locomotives. It was a time of appalling poverty in plenty and of poverty because of plenty. Activities in themselves highly serviceable, like raising pigs, or growing wheat and coffee, had become illusory inasmuch as these products were left rotting on the spot, were buried, or were used in really extrinsic ways —e.g., coffee in place of coal. This incredible experience of several years during which there was frightful destitution in the wealthiest nations in the world at the very time when real wealth was plentiful did more, I think, than the Russian Revolution to shape the destinies of the twentieth century. And I have a strong suspicion that there was a cause/effect relationship between the plenty of wealth and the extremes of poverty, as if by some enormous accident poverty came to be the specific result of an abundant production.

To know whether there are lasting causes for such occurrences is obviously important. But even assuming that the Great Depression was only a paradoxical and revolting accident, we are entitled to ask whether a labor force comes to produce illusory services because of the nature of what is produced or because of the ratio of what is produced to actual needs. To take the clearest example first, let us recall that opium, heroin, and other drugs are not always and under all circumstances harmful to human health. There is a medical use for both morphine and heroin. But how much pure morphine is needed for this purpose each year, say, for the 700,-000,000 people of China? I do not know, but I suspect that if the producers of opium in China had their way, on top of whatever quantity of opium is needed for medical use, they would produce indefinitely more opium to serve as an intoxicant for opium-smokers, -chewers and -drinkers. Here, then, is a well-known case in which even the most stubborn economist would grant that beyond a certain rate there is no real wealth produced, nothing actually serviceable to man but, on the contrary, something destructive.

What holds very clearly in the case of opium holds also, even if less clearly, in many other cases. For instance, fermented beverages serve genuine needs within certain limits, which are indeed relative to time and circumstances. These limits may not be easy to determine, but it is clear that producing wine, whiskey, or gin beyond whatever might be needed means that what is produced is no longer something serviceable but, on the contrary, something destructive. This case of alcoholic beverages is still rather simple, and in fact in most countries their production is more or less controlled in one way or another. But what about neckties, shirts, pajamas, stockings, and hundreds of other such articles in the production of which huge amounts of labor force and money are invested? Are the essential relations involved here not the same as in the case of opium or whiskey? Does not the production of these articles beyond a certain limit become instead of a service merely an empirical satisfaction of desires without genuine need? Yet these articles keep selling in the market and real wealth keeps leaking out of society. That is one aspect of the problem. The other aspect in which I am particularly interested is that, in such excessive production, work loses its character of social fruitfulness.

Let us return to the issue that has been basic in our consideration of the social aspects of work. We have seen that, over long periods in the evolution of human society (the present not excluded), most of its labor force has been kept in the margin of the community. The slaves and the laborers in the condition of servitude were simply not members of the civil community. In the case of the proletariat, we have a somewhat different situation, because these people have civil rights. They are owned by no one, and they may even enjoy political freedom. At the same time, however, their economic situation still drives them into forming a social class bent on secession. They too find themselves in the margin of society. Why?

In contrast to the slave, the modern wage-earner is legally an equal to his employer. He is his own master, and he enters with his employer into a contractual relationship. Under this contract something is sold for a compensation called a wage, and this something is work as such: plain and simple. But let us dare ask whether human work is something that can be bought and sold. Is human work really just another item of exchange? Is work like eggs, for which one gets money to be again exchanged for shoes? That is the question, and we shall try to view it from various angles until we have some sort of an answer.

We may as well begin with the notion of exploitation. "Exploitation" is a word which very frequently appears in revolutionary literature, especially in the literature pertaining to the revolt of the proletariat and representing the wage-earner as the victim. But what does it mean exactly? Beyond rhetoric, what is it that is expressed by this term? The answer, so far as I can see, is extremely simple: "Exploitation" in this context refers to an unequal exchange forced by circumstances upon the laborer. In the case of servitude, this is forced upon a man institutionally, but it is the same condition. For instance, Aristotle does his best to convince us that slavery is beneficial both to the master and to the slaves; he tries hard to make it look like an even exchange.[8] But of course slavery is beneficial principally to the master and only in a secondary way to the slave; the exchange is in fact unequal, and the slave is a victim of exploitation. Because equality is the fundamental law of exchange, an "unequal exchange" can be only one of two things: it may be a gift, if it is voluntary; if it is not a gift, it is exploitation. The latter may be institutional, as in the case of slavery, but it may also be imposed without any special institutions, as evidenced by the common practice of modern labor-relations, at least before the advent of labor unions. Unfortunately, there are still quite a few places in the world where a would-be wage-earner must simply accept whatever compensation he is offered for his service. Whether or not this compensation is equal to the service is something that he cannot even discuss. He has no choice. He must take the wage offered because he cannot afford to leave it. In such situations, the result more often than not is exploitation, and that is why such practices have been the main target in the protest of the working class from the early nineteenth century to our time. Described theoretically, the situation is one in which the compensation given as a wage is unequal to the service rendered. The difference is not a gift because it is not voluntary; therefore it must be a tribute extracted from the worker with the aid of circumstances. That is what we call exploitation, and, in spite of civil freedom enjoyed by the worker, it is definitely a species of servitude.[9]

[8] *Politics* 1.6.
[9] Cf. *Philosophy of Democratic Government*, pp. 230ff.

To make this clearer, let us assume now that the wage becomes equal to the service rendered. Is there still exploitation and servitude? I consider this question quite interesting. The problem is to decide whether in the case of the worker who is not economically independent, who has no machines, land, or property, a certain rate of compensation suppresses exploitation and relieves servitude. I am very much inclined to say "Yes," because I believe that there is something wonderful about an equal exchange. When, all other things being equal, the wage becomes equal to the service rendered, I think we have a condition of freedom. Is a secretary free from exploitation by the scholar for whom she works? In my opinion, it all depends on her salary. If it is one dollar an hour, no; if it is two dollars, perhaps. Between the case in which it is possible to speak of an equal exchange and the case in which the exchange is known to be unequal, there is a qualitative difference.

Now the best-known historical method for the exchange of goods has been the market, *piazza*, bazaar—that is, a place where multitudes of buyers and sellers meet to bargain with each other. Traditionally, this has been considered also the best method of obtaining an approximation to equality, which is the rule of commutative justice governing exchange. True or not, what we want to know is whether labor might not be an exception. Granted that equality in exchange of goods is often approximated in the market, what we want to know is whether trading labor in the market is also the best method of obtaining a fair wage? The theory of *laissez-faire* answers this question in the affirmative for one reason only: it considers human labor as just another commodity. Accordingly, the best way to find out how much this labor is worth is to have would-be workers bargain with would-be employers, just as farmers haggle with housewives over the price of chickens and vegetables. The market provides the same answer in either case. As Richard Cobden (1804–1865) put it, "When two employers are after a laborer wages go up, and when two laborers are after one employer wages go down." In the political economy of the great period of capitalist development, this principle was never questioned.

By the turn of the century, however, the view that labor cannot and must not be treated as an item of merchandise begins to gain ever wider acceptance, and a number of movements promoting what has been called "social justice" soon made this their basic tenet.[10] This is a rather confusing development, because the idea of social justice was already politically important in the 1880s. But there was never full agreement on all the things that it was supposed to mean. Now, on this one point, there was something like a consensus. Thus, at the end of the First World War, the Treaty of Versailles established in one section the League of Nations and in another (Part xiii) the International Labor Organization (ilo). Prominently included in the ilo charter was the principle that human labor was *not* an item of merchandise. Samuel Gompers was rumored to have had something to do with this, which might have well been true, because by 1919 that principle had been accepted all over the world by most diverse sections of opinion. But what does this principle mean? It asserts that labor, human work, must not be treated in the way that hogs, grain, chickens, or vegetables are treated. It asserts that labor is not just another commodity subject to the law of supply and demand. And it asserts that the just price of labor cannot be fixed by bargaining regardless of actual need. All this is clear, but that is not all there is

[10] In the United States, for instance, Theodore Roosevelt recognized not only that a wage-earner's labor was a "perishable commodity" but also that the labor problem was "a moral, a human problem" and that the workers were organizing to secure "not only their economic but their simple human rights." See *Theodore Roosevelt: An Autobiography* (New York: Scribners, 1908), pp. 470–471. See also Florence Kelley, *Some Ethical Gains Through Legislation* (New York: Macmillan, 1905).

to it. The principle that labor is not just another commodity introduces into economic thought and into social philosophy the all-important notion of distribution according to needs— another subject on which there has not been nearly enough discussion.

DISTRIBUTION ACCORDING TO NEEDS

Considering such problems as whether academic people are paid sufficiently for their services, whether high-school teachers can live on what they make, or whether the purchasing power of high industrial wages is really what it appears to be, the father of a large family has an understandable tendency to include in his calculation the large volume of goods he needs to maintain his family. Thus clearly in matters of wages and salaries, the case of a bachelor is strikingly different from that of the father of a family of six, eight, or twelve persons. But here again we have to reckon with the weight of received opinions. Who has not heard the slogan which is often phrased as a question: Does an employer pay a man for doing a certain job, or for bringing up children? This is another one of those idiotic clichés which appear to rest on sound evidential bases but in fact do not, and the sooner we get rid of them the better. Do you see what is behind this question? Sure enough, it is nothing else than the conception of human labor as a commodity all over again, the fiction that the only problem between employer and worker is the determination of the price of labor.

But is it true that we have only a single problem here? For example, suppose that a university needs one more physicist, and the administration has found two likely candidates. One is a good man, still young, who has a very good reputation but is not yet included among the great names of contemporary science. The other is a man of great experience, of tremendous achievements, who is also known for rare pedagogical qualities (it is said that J. Robert Oppenheimer, for instance, was able to develop in his students a veritable passion for the beauty of nuclear research). What is the administration to do? Clearly, in the second case a performance of a higher quality is expected and, strictly in terms of proper compensation for such service, a higher salary is indicated. So far this is a matter of exchange, resembling what goes on in the market place, where, assuming good faith, actual values of commodities are discussed with the purpose of reaching the best possible approximation to an equal exchange. But if what is being discussed is a man's salary or wage, can we stop here? I for one do not think so. Take two famous nuclear physicists, equally famous, or two beginning young physicists equally capable, but in both sets one is a bachelor, the other has eight children. Clearly, besides the problem of achieving an equal exchange, we have here a problem of compensation according to needs.

That our discussion is not purely academic can plainly be seen in the various practices devised by different societies in order to solve this problem. What are these practices? In this country, there are, for instance, deductions in computing one's income tax. Another practice which amounts to distribution according to needs, and which is becoming increasingly common throughout the world, is the principle of family allowances determined by the state. When I was serving in a French university as an employee with four children, I received automatically 4,200 francs on top of my salary. The total was not very much, because the salary was not really good. But the allowance was a substantial addition to my income, since it paid for more than half the rent of the kind of apartment that we needed. This practice is not restricted to universities. It is nation-wide, and the system works roughly as follows.[11] Regardless of the salaries they pay, all employers have to contribute to a general fund in proportion to the number of their employees and to the volume of their business. The family allowances for all workers are paid out of this fund, and so no employer is tempted to exclude a man with a large family because he might be more expensive to hire than a bachelor. To the employer it makes no difference; but it makes a difference to a man with a large family. Again, in this system, the employers' contributions have nothing to do with the ratio of bachelors in their employ; only the total number of employees counts. Nevertheless, from the fund established by these contributions, it is the employees with families who receive special allowances, and so their total wages consist of two parts. The first part certainly has the character of an ordinary wage, or price—i.e., it is a compensation paid in exchange for the services rendered. But the second part quite definitely embodies the principle of distribution according to needs.

Similar arrangements have been established by law in several countries, and apparently they work.[12] But would they work without law? Can these two principles—of equal exchange and of distribution according to human needs—operate entirely on the level of private relations? Is it possible in the absence of such a law for a would-be employee to tell a prospective employer something like this: "Of course, you realize that I shall require a larger salary than another man because with a family much larger than those of most of your employees, I could not possibly live on the salary which is

[11] See Wallace C. Peterson, *The Welfare State in France* (Lincoln: University of Nebraska Press, 1960).

[12] See the report on the *Conference on Labor Law in Europe* (London: British Institute of International and Comparative Law, 1962). See also Mark J. Fitzgerald, *The Common Market's Labor Programs* (Notre Dame, Ind.: University of Notre Dame Press, 1966).

sufficient for most of them"? To tell the truth, this is in effect what I told the University of Chicago when they kindly informed me that I would be welcome to join the faculty. By that time I had six children, none of whom was self-sufficient, which in 1948 was not so common in the faculties of the great universities. They hired me anyway, which shows that there are cases in which the principle of distribution according to needs, over and above the principle of equal exchange, may be affirmed in decisions arising entirely from private initiative and deliberation. But could such a system work smoothly in all cases without public regulation and without a huge consolidated fund managed by some public authority? In my opinion, that does not seem very likely.

Concrete consideration of public policy, however, is not our present purpose. Let us therefore turn immediately to the next theoretical problem, which to me seems decisive. Granted that human labor is not a commodity, and that there is much to be said for the principle of distribution according to needs, we face directly another issue which has not often been raised, at least not very loudly. To put it plainly, if human labor is not an item of merchandise, is anything just plain merchandise? After all, at the bottom of every problem of fair exchange of goods we find the problem of human labor, and a strong argument can be made that therefore nothing produced by human labor should be considered a mere commodity. Thus while the consideration that human labor is not an item of merchandise is a good starting point in the analysis of the relation of the worker to society, I do not think that we can stop there.

The point I have to make is rather simple. When a worker receives a wage unequal to the service rendered and has to accept it, we call that exploitation. But I remember from my childhood stories about the fishermen of my native province and how an abundance of herring could for them turn into a calamity. When many herring are after a few customers, it is the same as in the story of wages told by Cobden: the price of herring goes down. Is the fisherman, then, who has to make a living from his catch less exploited by low market prices than the worker by a wage unequal to his service? If human labor cannot be treated as an item of merchandise, then neither can herring, because the price of herring is the compensation for the service of the independent fisherman, just as the wage is the compensation for the service of the wage-earner. In the last analysis, whether we sell our ability to run a machine or our fish or vegetables, there is always the problem of obtaining a compensation equal to the service rendered, and the bargaining in the market may not be the best method of obtaining this equality.

In my view, recent historical developments are rather significant in this context. But the particular relation of wages and prices that we are interested in is not easily disengaged from history, and in order to do so I have to use a very rough outline. This outline may look like an oversimplification, but in my opinion it is not. The application to human labor of notions derived from the market place is definitely connected with the phenomenon of wage-earning, which becomes historically significant in the late eighteenth and early nineteenth centuries. By the time of the formation of the working class—that is, about the year 1848—the principle that human labor is just like any other commodity to be bought and sold in the market is the mainstay in the theory and practice of *laissez-faire* economics. But as it so often happens in history, various movements whose aspirations find expression in the call for "social justice" begin at about the same time to insist that human labor is *not* just another commodity. While differing on many other points, all these parties agree that human labor is not a piece of merchandise the price of which can best be determined in the market by the law of supply and demand. As already noted, this new principle was given official recognition in the charter of the ilo, and from that moment on, despite the continuation of old practices in many parts of the world, I see a definite trend in the evolution of ideas about social justice. This trend consists of introducing into the analysis of the market notions derived from what was at first considered to be the exceptional case of human labor. Clearly, a wholehearted denial that human labor is just another commodity could not leave the status of other commodities in the market unaffected. From now on, they too must be evaluated by humane and social standards.

I believe that this hypothesis can bring about some sort of order into that extremely confused but really deep development covered by the phrase "social justice." Irving Babbitt and a few other traditionalists have joked about the confusions of "social justice." [13] Their irony may be interesting, but it is not without reason that an extremely ambiguous expression like "social justice" asserts itself over such large portions of human society under such diverse circumstances. There must be something behind it, it must mean something. And one of the things it means, I believe, is a reversal of the practice of applying to human labor the rules derived from the market place. From now on, the market place will increasingly be judged by rules pertaining to human labor. Testing this hypothesis can do no harm; either it is verified, or it is not. But in testing it, I do not believe that anyone will have wasted his time.

In concluding what I have to say on the relation of work and wealth, I wish to add here a few words on the question of exchange *versus* free distribution. These remarks tie in with our recollections of the great world depression of the 1930s.

[13] See *Democracy and Leadership* (Boston: Houghton Mifflin, 1924), especially Chapter vi, "True and False Liberals."

That was a great event in modern history, an appalling situation in which tens and hundreds of millions all over the world acquired a revolutionary frame of mind. People became revolutionaries not because they did not want to suffer poverty; untold human generations had suffered poverty before, most often very quietly. But poverty becomes much, much less tolerable when it exists in the midst of plenty. Let us dare recall those days again. For instance, a lady who had been a school teacher at the time of Herbert Hoover and the Great Depression once told me how by ten o'clock in the morning they had to send children home, because the children were so weak, so depressed, and incapable of remaining attentive— they had had so little food. What drove many of the children's parents into revolt was that they knew well that the food was there. In other ages, after a great drought, if there was simply no food available people were not so unwilling to accept deprivation even for a long period. But when it is known that the wealth is there—that cows which would provide milk for these children are there and that they have been milked, but that the milk has been poured into the gutter— such a state of affairs creates a revolutionary situation, especially if there is suspicion that the very abundance of wealth is itself an additional cause of its not being available to all.

Rightly or wrongly, that is what men and women thought during the Great Depression, and I am sure that they were mostly right. In a great many cases, their services were unneeded precisely because the wealth was abundant. It was not only that wages were low, but that human labor was not in demand at all, and they had nothing else to bargain with in the market. In all such cases it is clear that abundance itself was a cause of poverty. How general this causality may be, how necessary or inevitable, is not certain. But this tragic experience should have opened our eyes to the immense fact that wealth can never be distributed adequately by means of exchange alone. As a matter of fact, at all times and in all societies, a considerable amount of wealth has to be distributed by methods distinct from exchange.

A few years ago, I had the privilege and the pleasure of being invited to teach summer school on the shores of Lake Tahoe. The seminar was organized by a California college and dedicated to social issues. Several positions were represented. Sidney Hook spoke for moderate socialism, another gentleman defended reasonable capitalism. Communism was represented by the only man of this school we could find, a very nice, friendly person who obviously did not know what it was all about. I was there to represent not any particular position but only what I had to say.[14] And one of the points I thought appropriate to make in those discussions of social philosophy was precisely that, in my opinion, distribution of wealth by way of exchange alone was impossible, and I also suggested that free distribution—that is, distribution of wealth without reciprocity—could play an important part in our society as it had in most other societies.

It goes without saying that I took all possible precautions against being misunderstood. For instance, I said plainly that I did not mean to deliver such distribution to the arbitrariness of individual good will; on the contrary, I specified that it was desirable that this free distribution be, as far as possible, institutionalized. Nevertheless, the reaction was as expected. Since we did not lecture but rather discussed our papers, and then the students wrote comments on our discussions, I soon got to read that my idea was absurd, that it was stupid and impossible. It seems that the phrase "free distribution" made most students think that I was proposing that people of means should simply sit at street corners and distribute

[14] Simon's paper was entitled "Social Justice." The seminar was organized by the College of the Pacific Philosophical Institute and took place in June 1950.—Ed.

money. Instead of trying to explain that they had completely misunderstood my point, I decided to wait.

The seminar lasted about four or five days, and toward the end I noticed that people began to realize that we were all meeting in halls lent by a Presbyterian organization; that we were all housed in lodgings belonging to the same organization; and that all we could say for or against "free distribution" was made possible by an obvious instance of free distribution. I could see that thought was beginning to stir, that there was a glimpse of the immensity of the processes of this kind that go on in our society and had prevailed in one fashion or another in most other societies. We were proceeding with the help of the Presbyterian Church, an independent organization. But the conference could have been organized by some agency of a welfare state. Personally, I prefer free distribution through independent institutions rather than directly through state institutions; but these are distinctions which can be made only according to the circumstances.[15]

Indeed, one thing I have been wishing for in my researches is an historical study of the institutional methods of free distribution of wealth throughout the ages of mankind. But in all the world, there is not a single book on this all-important subject. In the Middle Ages, at the time of the Renaissance, in the ancient cities and empires, there were plenty of laws and customs that provided for free distribution of many things. For instance, in long periods of what is called the Middle Ages, and in many countries, whoever lived next to a forest had an institutional right to collect wood from that forest for both building and heating purposes. That meant a great deal to the people, and it was clearly a process of free distribution, sanctioned either by law or at least by custom

[15] Cf. Yves Simon, *Community of the Free* (New York: Holt, 1947), especially the section on "Problems Worked Out by Socialism," pp. 153–165.

which was as powerful as law. There are a thousand facts of that kind which could be reduced to a finite number of types. How interesting it would be to have a book on that subject, if only to excite our imagination about the many alternatives to the extremely easy but perhaps destructive ways of state socialism.

6

Work and Culture

THE WHOLE OF THE PRECEDING DISCUSSION has been concerned
with putting together a complex definition of work. There is
no reason, therefore, to expect here a ready-made definition
of culture. Let us instead start with a general notion of culture, assuming that the word means something to all of us.
Then, in the course of our reflections on the relation between work and culture we shall try to be more and more
specific. In this way, we ought to be able to clarify at least
some of our present ideas about culture, and before we conclude our discussion we may even have a few elements of a
definition.

HISTORICAL ASPECTS

A number of things have been written about the valuation of
work and workers' life throughout the ages.[1] My feeling is

[1] A recent title is E. J. Hobsbawm, *Laboring Men: Studies in the History
of Labor* (New York: Basic Books, 1965).

143

that very little is known about it and that there is a tendency in these matters to indulge in oversimplification. Nevertheless, as long as we know what we are doing, there is nothing wrong with employing simplified ideas in a rough outline; qualifications can always be introduced as they are needed.

Let us then consider first the so-called "classical" societies. "Classical" is indeed an awfully vague term, and yet in regard to Greek history, for instance, all agree that it applies not to Homeric society but rather to the fifth century B.C. and to the age of Plato and Aristotle. Likewise, in the history of Rome, "classical" is used specifically to describe the century of Augustus, leading into the first century of Christianity. In modern European history, the term is applied most often to the seventeenth century, though the characterization "classical" might fit the entire period from the seventeenth century until quite recently (just how recently it is hard to say). Clearly, then, when we speak of classical societies we do not mean societies which are necessarily ancient but rather societies that belong to what are designated by our historical consciousness as the classical ages of Greece, Rome, and modern Europe.

In all these classical societies, there is a striking opposition between the life of work and the life of culture. The general idea of this contrast is well caught in the title of a book by a contemporary German philosopher, Josef Pieper, *Leisure: The Basis of Culture*.[2] In Aristotle, we find the same idea in a passage of the *Metaphysics* in which it is said that mathematics was invented by the leisure caste of Egypt.[3] Having plenty of leisure, the Egyptian priests succeeded in developing the first theoretical science—geometry—to an astonishing degree of perfection. This thesis is as familiar as it is plausible,

[2] Josef Pieper, *Leisure: The Basis of Culture* (London: Faber & Faber, 1952).
[3] *Meta.* 1.1. 981ʙ23.

but it just may be one of those oversimplifications that abound in interpretations of the relations between work and culture.

To begin with, Herodotus suggested that the Egyptians invented geometry because of a definite economic and social need. Every year when the floods came, boundary-markers throughout the valley of the Nile were destroyed, and surveys of property had to be repeated annually after the river returned to its bed.[4] Aristotle saw the connection between theoretical speculation and leisure; what he missed was the pressing socio-economic need which prompted that speculation. But why did Aristotle not see how extremely useful geometry was to the Egyptians? Is it because mixing theory with utility was contrary to his ideal of contemplative life? Perhaps. For Aristotle to know geometry was the main thing; to use it to mark property lines was incidental. Being a product of a classical age, so to speak, he did not value technical knowledge too much higher than manual work. And since most work was done by slaves in his time, he had an added reason to oppose such work to culture. All this sounds plausible and is close to the conventional interpretation of Aristotle's views. Yet it may not be the whole truth of the matter.

There is no question that Aristotle together with Plato minimizes the rational element in work, working man, and the working class of men. In the ninth book of the *Republic*, Plato asks "Why are mean employments and manual arts a reproach?" and answers, "Only because they imply a weakness in the higher principles."[5] Aristotle makes it even stronger and actually says that laborers operate as fire burns, except that fire burns by nature while a laborer operates by habit.[6] But this low valuation of manual labor in the first

---

[4] *Persian Wars* (New York: Modern Library, 1942), p. 109.
[5] *Rep.* 9.590.
[6] *Meta.* 1.1. 981ᴀ24.

book of the *Metaphysics* stands in sharp contrast to what Aristotle has to say about making things in book six of the *Ethics*. The capacity to make things, τέχνη, which is translated by *art*, is for Aristotle not just an habitual skill: it is what he calls an intellectual virtue. As he defines it, art is the ability to perform operations relative to a thing to be made, "involving a true course of reasoning." [7] But did Aristotle not see that the artisans who built the Acropolis must have had a good deal of such "art," even if they worked under the supervision of famous architects? How could he assume that they operated as fire burns?

To answer these questions some twenty years ago, I did not hesitate to say that in the development of his theory of intellectual virtues Aristotle was obviously inhibited by the contempt with which manual labor was looked upon in his society. But then one day I ran across a passage in the *Adventures of Ideas* which made me reconsider my views. Here is what Whitehead wrote:

The term Profession means an avocation whose activities are subjected to theoretical analysis, and are modified by theoretical conclusions derived from that analysis. . . . Thus foresight based upon theory, and theory based upon understanding of the nature of things, are essential to a profession.

The antithesis to a profession is an avocation based upon customary activities and modified by the trial and error of individual practice. Such an avocation is a Craft, or at a lower level of individual skill it is merely a customary direction of muscular labour.[8]

To illustrate the difference, let us take chemical engineering as a profession. When breakthroughs take place in the more

[7] *Eth.* 6.4. 1140ᴀ9.
[8] Alfred North Whitehead, *Adventures of Ideas* (New York: Macmillan, 1933), pp. 72–73.

theoretical branches of chemistry—in the science itself, so to speak, and most likely through pure research—chemical engineering will also be modified. That is a profession. What shall be taken as an example of craft? According to Whitehead's definition, we could take anything from making liquor by chewing corn, as was done by old women in Chile, to whatever the artisans of Aristotle did while building the Parthenon. The decisive point to be noted here is that, despite pressures of social opinion radically different from those that surrounded Aristotle, Whitehead makes as sharp a distinction between profession and craft as Aristotle ever made between τέχνη and ἐμπειρία. Whitehead is saying in effect that some individuals work as fire burns, by customary direction of muscular labor, and that this is quite different from the ability to do the same thing in a way that involves a true course of reasoning. This distinction then, over and above social reasons, appears to be well grounded in the nature of things. Whatever particular societies may think of people engaged in manual work—i.e., whether they be considered slaves or heroes— we understand that there are two ways in which manual work can be performed. The worker may direct his activities by his own technical knowledge, or he may rely exclusively on experience and physical skill.

None of this can change the fact that Aristotle did not particularly care for manual workers, but comparison of his theory with Whitehead's nevertheless helps to reduce the apparent contradictions between the *Metaphysics* and the *Ethics*. I think that the solution of the paradox is as follows. The purpose of the first chapter of the *Metaphysics* is to show that "all men by nature desire to know," that there is in man a deep desire to know things independently of all utility. In order to establish the existence of this disinterested desire, Aristotle compares empirical skill (ἐμπειρία) with art (τέχνη). So far as utility is concerned, art is not necessarily superior to experience, and it even sometimes happens that things done from experience are done better than things done from art. But still everybody concedes that art possesses an excellence of its own. What is it? Compared to experience, the excellence of art is its rationality. Insofar as a skill is an art, it comprises a grasp of the relation between the means and the end; art thus involves an apprehension of universal necessities in a "true course of reasoning." What Aristotle wants to show here is the activity of the theoretical intellect within practical thought itself, within rational processes directed, in this case, toward physical nature. And by following the manifestations of the theoretical intellect in an orderly sequence, Aristotle leads us to an understanding of the necessity of a science of the first causes and first principles. Art or technical knowledge is only a beginning; beyond it lies physics, and beyond physics, metaphysics. Ultimately, men just want to know.

I leave the classical age of Rome out of the picture, because I really do not know enough about it, and so we are again considering modern times. We may say that the modern classical age ended sometime in the nineteenth century when, following glorification of science (technical knowledge in our terms) by Saint-Simonists, poets started to sing about the glory of manual work. Yet we must not overlook a certain ambiguity in this development. The earliest "culture heroes" of this new age were the so-called captains of industry, hardworking and hard-driving industrialists. In fact, the entire bourgeois class to which they belonged was distinguished by the industriousness of its members. This was the Golden Age of the European bourgeoisie during which its members were dedicated to work, the administration of the life of work, the direction of manual labor. As the successor to the ancient aristocracy, however, and insofar as it imitated its predecessor, this bourgeoisie was at the same time becoming a leisure class which had to show, as conspicuously as possible, its freedom from work. I think that this conflict between the essentially industrious character of the modern middle class and its simultaneous tendency to conspicuous leisure in •imitation of the old aristocracy explains a number of developments in the history of modern societies.

My friend Jacques Maritain, who is not a social observer by vocation, has written in his books on the United States that, generally speaking, there is no bourgeoisie in this country.[9] The tendency to ape the aristocracy in its capacity of a leisure class appears here in the sort of person whom we call a *parvenu*, an upstart. In whatever may be called the real upper class in America, with the exception of an older and comparatively small section, there is no such tendency. The urge to conspicuous leisure is distinctly not American. Now, I think that Maritain is right. He himself is, as I am, a descendant of the aristocracy-aping French bourgeoisie, and he knows well its character. The European middle-class attitudes even today include a certain undervaluation of work, an inclination to dissociate work and culture and to set them in opposition to each other, and thus to consider freedom from work a praiseworthy evidence that the primary condition for culture has been realized. All other things being equal, this is not a typical American outlook. Of course, it can be found here and there in the United States, especially in the older society of the East and the South. But in the characteristically American agricultural and industrial societies of the Middle West, such an outlook is not typical. In Chicago or Milwaukee, the life of work and the life of culture are not so sharply separated. This means, all things considered, that there is no classical society in America, and perhaps there really never was one. Here, work has never been held in contempt or in irreconcilable opposition to culture. And that is also in part

* See *Reflections on America* (New York: Scribners, 1958).

the reason why a distinct proletarian class has never come into being here. Despite the simplification involved, a few key ideas like these can explain a lot of things historical and social.

In the present context, I should like to call attention to only one more historical aspect of the relation between work and culture. This has to do with the particular conditions of work created by modern industry. There is a famous page of Adam Smith on the manufacture of a pin, divided into seventeen operations, each performed by a different worker.[10] That was written in the eighteenth century, and of course the processes of division of labor have multiplied enormously since then. And all this time, moralists, sociologists, and literary gentlemen have kept complaining and being sentimental about the disastrous effects of this division of labor on man and society. These lamentations started at the very latest in the first quarter of the nineteenth century. I remember a paper by a man named Lemontey, which was considered a classic for generations.[11] It describes a situation so extremely familiar to us, the plight of the poor fellow who spends his days performing one of the innumerable operations into which the making of an article is divided in a modern factory, where except for the manager nobody has the picture of the complete process. This genre of social criticism has been remarkably constant. Only a few years ago a European sociologist of considerable reputation and real ability, whom I had known in my youth, happened to be visiting at the University of Chicago. He was to deliver a lecture to an audience composed mostly of people from the Committee on Social Thought, Department of Sociology, and Department of Economics, and he was advised to give his lecture on the highest

[10] *The Wealth of Nations* (New York: Modern Library, 1937), p. 4.
[11] Pierre Eduard Lemontey, *Oeuvres complètes* (Paris: Sauteley, 1829–1832). Attempts to trace this reference further have been unsuccessful.

possible level. But to me his talk seemed to be a repetition of what I had read in Lemontey before I was twenty years old. Here was a man very much up-to-date, who spent his time in Chicago visiting ultra-modern factories; but what he had to say was not much different from what was said by the moralists well over a hundred years ago. The message is always that extreme division of labor destroys human personality—and thus causes work to become removed farther than ever from culture.

I cannot help taking these sociological evaluations with a grain of salt. One reason may be that I have never worked in a factory. But I also know the background of the romantic imagination against which the phenomena pertaining to modern industry have been studied. The movement called "Romanticism" started early in Germany and then blossomed simultaneously in England, France, in this country, and to a degree in Italy.[12] Among a number of antinomic traits in this extremely ill-defined, complex development is its eulogy of an imaginary Middle Ages. Thus its adherents usually say that, while the medieval craftsman was a worker indeed, he was also an artist. If he was a shoemaker, he did not make one-fiftieth part of one shoe but a whole pair; if he was a maker of pins, he did not perform one-seventeenth of the process of making a pin, but rather he made the whole pin. And having an idea of the whole, he also had to reason about how to bring that whole into existence. He was a creator, and that is why in the work of the old artisans there is often great beauty. Furthermore, these craftsmen are said to have been possessed of remarkable conscientiousness and dedication, which gave their personalities an eminent integrity.

Some of these things, of course, may be true, but it is also

---

[12] Cf. Lilian R. Furst, *Romanticism in Perspective* (New York: St. Martin's, 1969), Appendix A, "Chronological Chart." See also F. L. Lucas, *The Decline and Fall of the Romantic Ideal* (New York: Macmillan, 1936).

a fact that they have been exaggerated by romantic writers—
for example, by E. T. A. Hoffmann (1776–1822). I remember one tale about a certain maker of barrels in Nuremberg
in the fifteenth century.[13] It is a lovely story about the master,
his craft, and his dedication to what is called his "masterpiece." "Masterpiece" originally meant a piece of work show-
ing that a man was no longer an apprentice but had mastered
his craft and was fully a craftsman; it was like, say, a master's
thesis and similarly respected. All of which is wonderful, except that these story-tellers never tell us the ratio of the working population engaged in such noble and cultivating work.
They seldom mention the large majority who had to toil at
such jobs as felling trees and splitting boards so that master
craftsmen could make tables, chairs, and barrels. What was
it like to cut a log into boards without a machine saw? It
must have been quite a job, both strenuous and time-consum-
ing. In comparing the modern and the medieval workers, let
us not forget those who in the fifteenth century were engaged
in very dull, very hard, and certainly not cultivating activities.
Because romantic writers have had great influence on the evolution of ideas about work and culture, special attention must
be called to these aspects so badly distorted in their stories.
After Hoffmann, John Ruskin (1819–1900) also became famous for contrasting the modern worker with the craftsman
of other ages, and he supplied many of those misleading ex-
aggerations that fill the literature on this subject. Here is a
representative sample:

A craftsman absolutely master of his craft, and taking such pride
in the exercise of it as all healthy souls take in putting forth their
personal powers; proud also of the city and his people; enriching,
year by year, their streets with loftier buildings, their treasuries
with rarer possessions; and bequeathing his hereditary art to a line

[13] *Meister Martin der Küfner und seine Gesellen*, in Hoffmann's *Sämmt-*
liche Werke, 14 vols. (Berlin: de Gruyter, 1922), vol. 2, pp. 153–221.

of successive masters, by whose tact of race, and honour of effort, the essential skills of metalwork in gold and steel, of pottery, glass-painting, wood-work, and weaving, were carried out to a perfectness never to be surpassed; and of which our utmost modern hope is to produce a not instantly detected imitation.[14]

But one may look at the modern conditions of labor also from another point of view. Everyone knows that one of the leading ideas of Henry Ford, in the early part of his career, was that in order to mass-produce automobiles cheaply it was necessary to organize work in such a way as to be served well by completely unskilled workers.[15] There are never too many skilled workers on the labor market, and they command high wages; so, in order to mass-produce automobiles cheaply, one must divide the process in such a manner that unskilled workers—peasants coming from Ireland, Poland, Portugal, Italy, or elsewhere—can do the job with a minimum of training and guidance. Despite what literary gentlemen say, this is extremely significant from a social standpoint. That is how ordinary people without any special skills happened to make good wages, perhaps for the first time in the history of mankind. This too is what distinguishes modern society from all past societies. Perhaps there are not many great artisans left in the world, but, to avoid the misleading implications of the romantic view of the modern times, all we have to do is to remember the people who had to prepare the material for Ruskin-like handicraftsmen. There is absolutely no doubt that in ancient ages a huge amount of human labor went into tasks that had very little to do with the culture of the human mind.

[14] *The Works of John Ruskin*, 36 vols., edd. E. T. Cook and Alexander Wedderburn (London: Allen, 1908), vol. 34, pp. 353–354.

[15] See Keith Sward, *The Legend of Henry Ford* (New York: Rinehart, 1948), Ch. IV. See also Henry Ford, *My Life and Work* (New York: Garden City, 1922), and Allen Nevins, *Ford: The Times, The Man, The Company* (New York: Scribners, 1954).

Along with the foregoing remarks on typical attitudes toward work in classical societies, on the paradox of opposition between work and intellectual virtue in Aristotle, and on the absence of a society of the classical type in the United States, this should suffice by way of an historical introduction.

CULTURE AND CIVILIZATION

Next, let us approach our subject analytically. We have no ready-made definition, but there are common notions about what culture means, which we can use to begin to work toward a definition. Again, I do not promise that we shall be able to put one together, but it may be enough if we get started on the right track.

"Culture," *cultura* in Latin, was already used in its present derived meaning in ancient times. Originally, it referred to the cultivating of the soil. There is a difference between a field where things grow wild, and where by luck we may find a few plants useful to man, and a field cultivated with the purpose of obtaining a harvest over and above what nature would produce if left to itself. When we transfer this idea to the case of man, we understand very well that what we mean by culture is not something produced by nature but something superadded to the effects of nature by the agency of the human will and reason. The expressions "physical culture" and "physical education" are quite significant here. When we observe how far primitive people are from being able-bodied, we understand that in order to obtain the proper development of muscles alone and a proper balance of muscles and other components of the human body, it is necessary for the body to be educated and cultivated; such results are not obtained by just letting nature take its course. Clearly, then, the general notion of culture refers to rationally controlled processes. But the word is used in a wide range of senses, from the extremely vague and all-embracing to those which are rather narrow and perhaps arbitrarily restricted. Let us consider a few accepted meanings.

The broadest meaning of culture is to be found in anthropology and ethnology. Ethnologists and anthropologists speak of the culture of the Tasmanians just as they speak of the culture of the Mayas, the Chinese, or the British. They mean by culture anything and everything added by human initiative to the biological results of human existence. Thus the use of extremely crude pottery would be a culture-phenomenon just as definitely as are the tragedies of Shakespeare. This meaning is firmly established in ethnology today, and there is no use trying to change it. But we should be aware that when we speak of the culture of the Chinese, the word does not have exactly the same meaning as when we speak of the culture of the Tasmanians. For instance, when we ask "How much culture did Marco Polo find in China?" we do not mean the same thing as when we ask "How much culture was there in Tasmania when the island was first discovered?" In the latter case, we definitely use a much broader meaning.

Among the diverse meanings of the word "culture," especially in regard to the contrast in amplitude and restriction, I call attention to possible opposition between the notions of culture and civilization. This idea was conceived toward the end of the nineteenth century by the Germans and was later adopted by the Russians.[16] "Culture" in this conception has a favorable meaning, "civilization" a pejorative one. Culture is all that expresses life, genuineness, and spontaneity, while civilization includes much that is artificial, mechanical, and contrived. This is a particularly grave distinction, because we cannot change the etymology of "civilization." In many cases

[16] Jacques Maritain, *True Humanism* (New York: Scribners, 1938), p. 88. "Religion and Culture," in *The Social and Political Philosophy of Jacques Maritain*, edd. Joseph W. Evans and Leo R. Ward (New York: Scribners, 1965), pp. 217–218.

the origin of a word may be lost, but that is not the case of "civilization." The root of this word is *civis*, citizen. Taken seriously, then, such contrast between culture and civilization would imply that what pertains to man as a citizen is something artificial or mechanical, rather than genuine and spontaneous. For instance, legal relationships would thus be relegated to civilization, to the domain of the contrived, at a far remove from what is alive and personal to man, and culture in its relation to law would change from something that develops from within men to something that is imposed on them from the outside.

That these matters are awfully confused is precisely the point: we must be aware of the power of confused ideas. Jacques Maritain, in noting this contrast between "culture" and "civilization" in a number of German and Russian writers, warns the reader that he will not make any such distinction. The interesting question, however, is whether this contrast pertains only to these particular philosophies of life and society or whether it could be significant independently of their specific postulates. In those passages in which Maritain declares that he himself will make no distinction between "culture" and "civilization," he obviously implies that the contrast is not relevant except from a rather specific philosophic position. But I see a problem here.

On the one hand, it is obvious that the notion of civilization comprises the whole system of legal and political relations in any given society. If the word has any meaning, it certainly includes, among other things, the whole range of relations embodied in constitutions, laws, and legal and political practice. But can it be said, on the other hand, without being somewhat arbitrary, that legal and political relations belong specifically to culture? I do not think so, unless "culture" is understood in the all-embracing meaning of the ethnologists (which is another problem). We all agree that culture is more or less connected with civilization and therefore with the legal and political system of a particular society.[17] But take the example of the French. So far as culture is concerned, they consider themselves first in the world (they of course exaggerate a little). Yet, so far as their constitutional and political practices are concerned, I do not think that they even pretend to distinction. Here is a striking discrepancy which I consider significative as well as significant. There is apparently something we call "culture" that can be possessed eminently by a society while the civic relations of that society are by no means remarkable. Since the latter are determinant of civilization, we may have here a hint of opposition. This, I think, holds independently of the more or less dubious views of the contrast between what is spontaneous and what is artificial in human and social life, alleged by some to be embodied respectively in culture and in civilization.

THE HARD CORE OF CULTURE

This discussion of the meanings of the word "culture" has been indispensable in preparation for an analysis of the thing itself. Again, we are not taking "culture" in the broad sense of the anthropologists and ethnologists. Moreover, we have in mind primarily intellectual culture rather than moral culture. There are people of excellent morality who have no sense for poetry or painting or sciences, and who may even lack good manners. We describe such people as uncultured, although we respect them for their moral excellence. On the other hand, there exist also supercultured people who have sunk to the bottom of moral debasement. They are sometimes called sophisticated, but, needless to say, even if we here mean by "culture" primarily what pertains to intellectual

[17] Cf. Jacob Burkhardt, *Force and Freedom*, ed. James Hastings Nichols (New York: Meridian, 1955). See also Raymond Williams, *Culture and Society* (New York: Columbia University Press, 1958).

excellence rather than to moral qualities, that does not mean that we are overly impressed by this kind of person.

To start this discussion of intellectual culture, it seems best to begin with what is structural in it. I use "structural" here in a metaphorical sense derived from the way in which we speak of a building, because I conceive of this structural component of culture to be like a frame that supports it. For instance, in Aristotle's theory of culture this structural frame is found in two works: in book six of the *Ethics* and in the *Posterior Analytics*. Now, *Analytica Posteriora* is a great and difficult treatise on logic, which from the beginning to the end seems concerned with nothing but the logic of demonstration, and this has lead some to hold that for Aristotle intellectual culture is something exclusively theoretical and highly abstract. In this view we have one of those stubborn errors known as half-truths; but, to get the whole truth, we have merely to turn to book six of the *Ethics*, where Aristotle treats of the intellectual virtues. In my view, these intellectual virtues constitute an integral part of Aristotle's theory of culture and may indeed be considered its foundation.

"Intellectual virtues" is an expression which has been injected into the veins of American academic life by Robert M. Hutchins. At the beginning of his presidency at the University of Chicago in 1929, he somewhat shocked the academic world by asking, point-blank, what the purpose of higher education was. Was it to turn out superbiological organisms, wonderfully adjusted to life in society, or was it to develop intellectual virtues? While this controversy still swirls around us, Mr. Hutchins has staunchly persevered in his view that the latter is the only legitimate purpose of higher education.[18] But what are these intellectual virtues?

[18] See Robert M. Hutchins, *The Higher Learning in America* (New Haven: Yale University Press, 1936), and *The Learning Society* (New York: Praeger, 1968).

According to Aristotle, the intellectual virtues are understanding, science, wisdom, art, and prudence, and before we go on, let us make sure that we know what each of them means.[19]

The first intellectual virtue, νοῦς, is translated by W. D. Ross as "intuitive reason."[20] I prefer "understanding," not only because it is closer to tradition, but because "reason" is essentially discursive—as in Hamlet, "a beast that lacks the discourse of reason."[21] To speak of intuitive reason, therefore, is somewhat contradictory; if reason is taken properly, it is not intuitive, and intuition is not discursive. At the same time, the faculty by which we perceive the truth of immediate propositions is what we call understanding. These definitions, or more exactly definitional propositions, do not need a middle term to manifest their truth. They simply state that *this* is the definition of *this* subject. If we know what we are talking about (for instance, if we know what "whole" and "part" mean), such propositions are understood without demonstration; they are antecedent to any possibility of demonstration (viz., "a whole is greater than any one of its parts"). We clearly cannot demonstrate that a subject has a certain property, if we do not know what that subject is. And to express our knowledge of what a subject is, we need definitional propositions worked out by the faculty called "understanding." My final reason for preferring this word to "intuitive reason" is in order to keep, as in Greek, the same word for intellectual power itself and for this most fundamental faculty by which those propositions are understood, which having no middle term are above mediation and demon-

---

[19] The order of discussion in book six of the *Ethics* is not the same as here. The chief intellectual virtues, as named by W. D. Ross, are taken up by Aristotle as follows: scientific knowledge, art, practical wisdom, intuitive reason, and philosophic wisdom.

[20] *Ethics* 6.6

[21] *Hamlet*, Act I, scene ii.

stration. Aristotle's word, νοῦς, also means "mind" in Greek. Is this ability to understand immediate propositions just a part of intellectual culture or an indispensable foundation of it? The answer is that it is the foundation, for, while it may not be in act prior to experience, understanding is certainly in act prior to the cultivation of the intellect. An extremely uncultured person may possess understanding, sometimes even to a considerable degree. In fact, we find some rather refined people who say, "If two plus two equals five on the moon, I have no objection," and we find uncultured people who object. Aristotelian philosophy is here on the side of the latter, because they have retained their understanding of immediate propositions: two plus two does not equal five—all other things being equal. The reservation is necessary because of the strange things going on in mathematics in our time. Today it could be easily demonstrated that a square can be a circle, and vice versa, by simply shifting from one system of postulates when speaking of circles to another system of postulates when speaking of squares. But these mathematical procedures do not contradict the understanding of basic propositions.

We shall call the second intellectual virtue, ἐπιστήμη, "science" rather than "knowledge," because the latter term may refer both to the intellectual and to the sensory.[22] Science, in this Aristotelian sense, is the intellectual quality by virtue of which the mind is at ease in the field of demonstrable conclusions. The third intellectual virtue, wisdom, σοφία, is a particular case of science.[23] We shall not treat it as a separate virtue, though as a science it has a character of supremacy and is also called by Aristotle metaphysics, first philosophy, and theological science or science of things divine

[22] *Ethics* 6.3.
[23] *Ethics* 6.7.

—that is, those beyond the world of motion. This science which is concerned with the first causes and the first principles enjoys a unique privilege insofar as organization is concerned, for one of its functions is to set the whole universe of knowledge in order. Setting things in order is what we expect of a wise person; a wise person is not necessarily one who knows a lot but rather one who puts everything in its proper place. The science which enables him to do so is called wisdom.

The fourth intellectual virtue, art or τέχνη, is, as we have already learned, the intellectual quality which renders a man at ease in the domain of things to be made,[24] while the fifth and last intellectual virtue, prudence, renders him at ease in the domain of actions to be done.[25] For the latter there are difficult problems pertaining to either my personal conduct or to my behavior as a member of a group, or to what I must do as a leader of a group. To solve these problems one needs a distinct intellectual quality which Aristotle calls φρόνησις. This is translated by W. D. Ross as "practical wisdom." But even though the meaning is correct, I still prefer to call it "prudence" because Aristotle's term has for centuries been translated by the Latin *prudentia*.

These five virtues represent, in my view, the core of the intellectual culture in Aristotle. But are they really virtues, properly speaking? Robert M. Hutchins called them intellectual virtues, and this usage is supported by a long line of precedents beginning with Aristotle himself, who calls these things ἀρεταί, which indeed means virtues. Yet if we consider carefully the definition of virtue in book two of the *Ethics*, we realize that it does not apply to all these qualities, because virtue strictly speaking includes rightness of use. For instance, it is not easy to see how a person could make a wrong use of

[24] *Ethics* 6.4.
[25] *Ethics* 6.5.

the virtues of justice or temperance by employing them against their purpose.[26] In fact, that is absurd and contradictory, because to have the virtue of temperance is to possess a quality which guarantees the right use of the virtue itself. The same, however, cannot be said, without qualification, of art or of science, and so we have a problem here.

There is in the *Ethics* a passage which annually drove at least one student in the Committee on Social Thought to my office, and the first time this happened I was seriously embarrassed. The passage is translated by W. D. Ross as follows: "But further, while there is such thing as an excellence in art, there is no such thing as excellence in practical wisdom." [27] What could that mean? I suspect Ross did not try to find out, otherwise he would have produced a better translation. He is a great translator, among the very best—which simply indicates the difficulty of these matters. What he translates by "excellence" is ἀρετή, so that if we translate literally we have, "There is virtue in art, and there is no virtue in prudence." But still, what does that mean? Something frightfully simple: It means that having mastered an art, one still needs virtue in order to make proper use of his art; whereas if one has the virtue of prudence, or practical wisdom, he already possesses the principle of good use and needs nothing else to apply it rightly in action.

So we arrive at the strange conclusion that of the above five qualities only one is a virtue in the full sense, and that is the one which is not purely intellectual. In other words, there is really no such thing as an "intellectual virtue." But if we want to blame anyone for this curious usage, we must not blame Robert M. Hutchins. It is really Aristotle's own fault. He was a thinker who, when he needed extreme precision of language, provided it; but on the next page when extreme

[26] *Ethics* 2.4; 3.10.
[27] *Ethics* 6.5. 1140B20–25.

precision was no longer required, he no longer cared. A virtue properly so-called is moral virtue—that is, a state of character or a stable quality which, by definition, procures its own good use. Understanding, science, wisdom, and art are not of that nature, because they are indifferent to the use to which they may be put. With his immortal naïveté, Aristotle remarks that the grammarian is the man best qualified to make grammatical mistakes, if he wants to tease. For us, a chemical engineer is the logical choice for sabotaging a chemical plant.

The conception of the structural in intellectual culture which I want to propose here is closely related to these so-called intellectual virtues of Aristotle. Excluding the understanding of first principles, which is natural rather than cultural, we have science, wisdom, prudence, and art left, and, as we have just noted, only one of these—i.e., prudence—is a virtue unqualifiedly. But whatever these things may be, I believe that it is possible to demonstrate convincingly that they constitute the structural part of culture. Structure of course does not mean the whole. If our dwellings were reduced to their frameworks we would be at a severe disadvantage, and we could hardly call them dwellings. Likewise, a notion of culture restricted to what is structural in it may not correspond to anything that would look like a satisfactory definition of culture. There is a lot more to culture than just structure, and we shall get to it soon enough. But if science, wisdom, art, and prudence which make up the structural component of culture are not "intellectual virtues," what are they?

In my opinion, a better name for these intellectual qualities is habitus, rather than virtues. But this name must be traced to a different root-meaning than is commonly supposed. In most books, that word, *habitus* in Latin, is translated with etymological crudity as "habit." Yet when a truly precise meaning is needed, "habit" is worse than useless, because it means exactly the contrary of "habitus." This is why I have been struggling for thirty years for the acceptance of the word habitus in the vernacular. It makes no sense to call our five virtues intellectual habits. In the history of science, habits of thought have been mistaken all too frequently for objective necessity. For instance, in a civilization in which it has always been taken for granted that there is no alteration in celestial bodies, it will be considered axiomatic that celestial bodies are incorruptible. I do not know whether it started with the Babylonians or much earlier, but I know that this habit lasted until the seventeenth century and was broken only when Galileo with his telescope was able to show stars whose qualitative appearances changed.[28] This is one example among a thousand, and the same is evident in the history of moral ideas. How often have rules of action been held axiomatic, when as a matter of fact they were merely customs that had never been subjected to rational analysis? How often indeed have such social customs been at variance with conclusions of rational analysis? We all know that such instances have been all too frequent in history, and they all point to the difference between the kind of necessity which proceeds from habits of thought and the kind of necessity which proceeds from objects of thought. The despairing skepticism of Hume consists precisely in saying "There is no objective necessity, all you can find in the mind is the subjective necessitation of habit." [29] Thus, to call *science* an intellectual habit is to miss what is essential in it—namely, the search for and (in the best cases) the grasping of a necessity which is not the effect of repetitive activity of the mind but the expression of what constitutes a

[28] See Yves Simon, *The Great Dialogue of Nature and Space*, ed. Gerard J. Dalcourt (Albany, N.Y.: Magi, 1970), pp. 4–9.

[29] *A Treatise of Human Nature*, Book I, Section XIV, "Of the Idea of Necessary Connexion": "Upon the whole, necessity is something, that exists in the mind, not in objects; nor is it possible for us ever to form the most distant idea of it, considered as a quality in bodies" (*The Philosophy of David Hume*, ed. V. C. Chappell [New York: Modern Library, 1963], p. 112).

form of being. In widely different ways, there is also objective necessity in *art* and in *wisdom,* and that is why these things are, if not virtues in the full sense of the term, still something greatly different from mere habit. They are qualities which owe their character of certainty to being grounded in a necessity of an objective nature.

To get back to our etymological argument, let us note that there is among philosophers some controversy about the translation of Aristotle's ἕξις. This noun is related to the verb ἔχειν which means "to have," and came into Latin, perhaps through Cicero, as *habitus,* related to *habere.* Cicero was a great popularizer of Greek philosophy who, though not always profoundly understanding, did a lot of vocabulary work. His *habitus* is a good translation from the Greek original: it has something to do with "to have." But why is there no exact equivalent of this term in modern philosophical language? I believe that the notion expressed by that word was lost sight of in the seventeenth century at the time when philosophical vernaculars were taking shape. We would not expect to find a word like that in Descartes, who has no use for intellectual *habitus,* so to speak, because he has his four rules of method. Nor would we expect to find it in Hobbes, another mechanist though of a different stripe. Yet these two were the first great philosophers writing in the vernacular, with the result that *habitus* was never translated from the Latin. Somebody once told me that in an obscure seventeenth-century French writing, *habitus* is rendered by *ayance* which is related to *ayant,* the present participle of *avoir.* That is a lovely word, but I do not think that it could be revived. At any rate, it would not give us a solution in English, for I cannot think of a coinage related to "having" that would do the job. So what is left for us to do is to use the Latin term, *habitus,* with its original meaning, in English. ("Habitus" is in fact found in unabridged English dictionaries, though not in our sense but rather referring to the general disposition of an organism, the sense in which it is used in medicine.)

This apparent semantic digression on the etymology of habitus has been quite intentional. My point is that in the intellectual habitus—whether of the contemplative type as in science and wisdom, or of the productive type as in art, or of the active type as in prudence—there is a stable quality which is essentially relative to an objective necessity. By this I do not mean that, for instance, everything taught in a scientific department at a university is objectively necessary. What goes on there under the name of science is to a very large extent made up of factual information, educated opinion, and probability; yet this aggregate owes its existence to a nucleus of hard, objective necessity, to which it is connected by the scientific habitus. Likewise, though we speak of miracles of production and of relativity in moral judgments, we know that neither of these activities admits of complete arbitrariness. A core of objective necessity supports our achievements in arts and prudence as well as in science. That is what really matters for the understanding of habitus as the structural component of culture. But this insight is also decisive for the understanding of the relation between work and culture.

In the early part of our analysis of the concept of work, we set in contrast to what we called activities of legal fulfillment certain other activities which we said expressed free development. To go to a coffee shop for a cup of tea because one has just met an old friend with whom it is pleasant to chat is not the same as to rush in for a cup of tea because one has been exposed to bad weather and hopes that drinking something hot may prevent a cold. The latter action pertains to legal fulfillment, the former to free expansion. Now, intellectual habitus clearly represent activities of legal fulfillment. In them there is no fancy, no frills, no jokes; they, like work, pertain to what is serious in human life. Stable and certain, because they are built on objective necessity, they are capable of constituting the structural in culture, its hard core. But as life is not all work, we cannot have a theory of culture without postulating also a lot of activities of free development independent of objective necessity. Indeed, some think that such activities are precisely and exclusively what constitutes culture, what culture is. We want to examine this matter closely, and we want to pay special attention to the alleged opposition between this unnecessary, subjective, free aspect of culture and what we have just identified as its hard core.

THE PLENITUDE OF CULTURE

An important element in the contrast between the component of free expansion in culture and its hard core of legal fulfillment has been expressed by Jacques Maritain in a single sentence which I am eager to quote in the original because it is as nicely phrased as it is profound. Maritain writes: *"Les gens du monde, polis sur toutes les faces, n'aiment pas l'homme à habitus avec ses aspérités."* [30] I read that thirty years ago and could never forget it. *Les gens du monde* are the "beautiful people," the society people who go to parties but also support and participate in what are called cultural activities. They are *polis sur toutes les faces*: very polished in their ways; but they *n'aiment pas l'homme à habitus*: they do not love the man possessed of habitus; *avec ses aspérités*: with, or rather because of, his roughness.

I am not completely sure that Maritain foresaw all the consequences of his remark, but it captures the truth of the matter precisely because it reveals the ruthless character of objective necessity. It is quite possible that a man of distinguished intellectual habitus, like a man of distinguished morality, may

---

[30] See *Art and Scholasticism*, trans. Joseph W. Evans (New York: Scribners, 1962), p. 12.

not be what is called "polished." There are great men of science who lack manners, and there are great artists who are rather notorious for their boorishness, which may be cultivated to some extent but is not entirely artificial. In fact, such traits seem to belong to personalities excellently developed with regard to some habitus, or virtue, be that mathematics or courage, the art of painting or justice. We may go even further and ask: Could a good philosopher be a boor? I am not sure, but I doubt that a philosopher strictly limited to his habitus would be a very creative philosopher. What is certain, though, is that neither his philosophical habitus nor all the virtues that he might possess would of themselves suffice to make him a cultured person. To be that he would have to be able to make also some contribution through activities of free expansion.

Thus while a relation to objective necessity lies at its core, there is in culture also something that for the moment we may designate by a metaphorical expression. We may compare it to a flower, or to a field of flowers, or to a bouquet of flowers. The use of metaphors in philosophy proper must either be rejected or at least strictly controlled; but in the phase of discovery, in the introduction to a subject, nothing is more natural than to use metaphors. In fact, a rich metaphorical imagination is an indispensable privilege of all creative philosophers. Philosophy will begin when the metaphor is transcended, but in the introduction to philosophy we have to use metaphorical analogies. Now as far as culture is concerned, we all see in it something that we should like to compare to flowers, to blooms; we see that something not as root or trunk, not even as fruit. We see it as a bloom, and I believe that this is so precisely because we feel that flowers represent something that in some way escapes and transcends necessity.

The reason I am staying in the realm of metaphorical expression is that we are touching here upon a metaphysical problem of the first magnitude, which has not been very well studied. Let us, therefore, proceed by way of seemingly trivial observations about daily life. For instance, it is perfectly sensible to divide a family budget into, on the one hand, "necessities," such as food, clothing, and shelter, and, on the other, such things as recreation, luxuries, even "whims." The latter are not determinately necessary, but all observers of human nature and of society agree that those things are perhaps even more indispensable to human beings than a certain minimum of calories per day. Well-to-do people are often scandalized when they see the poor people to whom they give money spend part of it feeding dogs or cats or birds. This is surely significant: people would rather share an insufficient food ration with a bird than not have something unnecessary in their daily life. Social workers who do not understand this are not very intelligent. It is too general a fact not to mean something and, indeed, it is philosophically quite intelligible. All we have to do to grasp it is to realize that a rational nature involves the paradox of a system of necessities open to infinity. When we say "nature" we mean something definite, but when we say "rational" we posit a nature which over and above its definite needs enjoys an openness to infinity.

This paradox is not merely human: it is universal. Look around in the universe. Superabundance and luxury prevail throughout the world of our experience. An animal psychologist, who was both philosophically and romantically inclined, remarked to me once that in the spring the birds sing far more than is allowed by Darwinian theory. In order for the species to survive, the cock need not sing so much; a few sounds are enough to attract the attention of the female. But the birds sing a hundred times more than is needed for the purposes of the species.

Along the same line of thought, we may well wonder at all those strange shapes in the zoo. Is there any determined necessity that there be such a multiplicity of species of apes, felines, reptiles, birds, and so on, all of which we are so eager to preserve? Notice how nervous we feel when we read that there are perhaps two dozen whooping cranes left in the world, and that some minor accident could cause their total disappearance. But what if the species did disappear? This would not interfere with any of our fellow human beings, it would in no way jeopardize our society. It would not be half as grave as a recession, and a slight rise in unemployment would be something much more important to worry about. And yet, there is genuine concern for the whooping crane and willingness to make an effort to preserve the species. It is as if at the metaphysical bottom of our hearts we have a sense—obscure perhaps but very strong—for the irreplaceable worth of something that has the character of a flower. Indeed, there is a kind of extravagance not only in the human world but also in the universe at large.

What I am trying to show is that as we look for what is most firm, profound, and certain in culture, we find the intellectual habitus. Yet they are rough and ruthless, and whatever in human life or human culture resembles flowers or the excessive singing of the birds in the spring is not to be found in them. Thus to have intellectual habitus gives one only a foundation of culture but certainly not the whole of it. What is needed to have the fullness of culture is something more, something that in some way is above necessity, is independent of need, and is fulfilling no laws except perhaps its own. Put metaphorically, we may say, then, that there is no culture without flowers. But put objectively, we should say that culture requires activities of free expansion because they express the plenitude of the nature of rational beings. Either way, what still remains to be carefully examined is the relationship between these free activities and the objective necessity found in intellectual habitus.

In my view, the decisive question is best put as follows: Is there any way for the intellectual habitus, grounded as they are in objective necessity, to enter into the world of free expansion, superabundance, and unnecessariness? As explained above, the three intellectual habitus that we have found to be relevant to the theory of culture are *science*, *art*, and *prudence*. We leave out understanding which we said is natural; and we include wisdom in science. Let us also recall briefly that science, ἐπιστήμη, is the intellectual quality that sets the mind at ease with demonstrable conclusions; that art, τέχνη, is the intellectual quality that makes us at ease with things to be made; and that prudence, φρόνησις, is the intellectual quality that renders man at ease in the realm of action. Our question, then, is whether in science, art, and prudence, or in any of them, it is possible to move on into the realm of freedom and fancy—to cultivate flowers, as it were. This is not an easy question to answer, and what I have to say on it is only tentative.

In regard to science, I feel fairly certain that the answer must be in the affirmative, ultimately because of the uselessness of the scientific achievement. Here we are of course not considering science as a source of technology but rather as pure research, that is, as an intellectual habitus. It also goes without saying that this science, aimed at the excellence of knowledge, is "useless" in a way which is not synonymous with the lack of worth or value. We have already explained that in utilitarian schools of thought the good is the useful and what is useless is not good. But we always have to ask, "Useful for what?" The useful is essentially conducive to something, and it is really not intelligible unless understood in relation to a good of a terminal character. In the last analysis, utilitarianism is an impossible philosophy; to justify it, its proponents must surreptitiously reintroduce terminal goods like biological survival or pleasure, for by definition the useful cannot be terminal. So when we speak of the "uselessness" of pure science, notice, please, that here the suffix "-ness" does not indicate a privation but rather the transcendence of a state of imperfection. Because of this transcendence, I would affirm that for the scientific mind there is an opening into the world of free expansion.

To take an example, let us look at modern mathematics. Today leading mathematicians find it rather difficult to explain what they are doing or why. I remember André Weil, reputedly one of the greatest mathematicians of our time, saying, "Yes, we do things like that, and if we are asked 'Why?' we have a perfect right to answer, 'We do it because it amuses us.'" There might be a social question here—who should support any part of mathematics whose only excellence consists in the amusement it provides for the mathematicians?—but the word "amusement" in this context obviously conveys something more profound than in the ordinary usage. In fact, it represents that opening into the world of free expansion which is characteristic not only of mathematics— where independence of axioms proceeds from very particular causes[31]—but of all really advanced theoretical thinking.

Another example is found in the work being done in logic today. From the layman's point of view, it is extremely discouraging that the logicians either do not want to or cannot explain what is going on in modern logic. The reason of course is not that our logicians are vicious or irresponsible. The present situation is rather a result of the fact that in this century logic has developed in all directions, and there is no human mind powerful enough to command all these fantastic developments. At the time of Kant, the basic rules of formal logic developed by Aristotle had not changed much; those were happy days for both the layman and the logicians, with

[31] See Yves Simon, "Nature and the Process of Mathematical Abstraction," *The Thomist*, 24, No. 2 (April 1965), 117–139.

such a simple history of the discipline. But in our time, and rather suddenly, formal logic has expanded into many new directions, some of which are still unknown because they are indicated in manuscripts which nobody has read. Yet the few works that have been read suffice to give us an idea of the multiplicity of developments since, say, the day of Augustus De Morgan, George Boole, Bertrand Russell, and A. N. Whitehead. In the present situation, it seems that all one logician has to say to another is "I do not follow you," implying "I do not care about what *you* do." This is indeed embarrassing, because if there is a discipline which should facilitate communication it is logic. But what many modern logicians seem to have forgotten is that logic, though a science in its own right, is relative to the service of other sciences. This is the main reason for their scattering in all possible directions. While being quite scientific, a good deal of work is done in logic today which is not logically useful.

Modern logic and modern mathematics illustrate in a particularly striking fashion the possibility of transcending objective necessity in science. Recent developments in both these disciplines have been in the nature of free expansion rather than in the nature of legal fulfillment. We can see clearly how, as soon as utility is transcended, and the scientific mind has nothing else to do but search for truth, there is for it an escape into luxury, extravagance, plenitude—yes, even infinity. I believe that this possibility is not limited to logic and mathematics but is present in all science.

In regard to prudence, however, I am quite sure that the question of the possibility of free expansion must be answered in the negative. Unlike the achievements of science, the judgment of prudence is always about something useful, and moreover it is useful in relation to something unqualifiedly necessary. What prudence as an intellectual habitus assures to those who possess it is nothing less and nothing more than the proper action at the right time for the given circumstances. True, this judgment may be that the thing to do is to go on a vacation, play chess or tennis, or take a nap; but a prudential judgment leading without fail to prudent action always retains the character of something useful relative to something necessary. Under any and all conceivable circumstances, it is necessary to do that which is right, and, even though the decision may be to relax or to abstain from action, I do not see in prudence as an intellectual habitus any possibility of escape into the world of free development. The prudent man cannot do as the bird which sings more than it is allowed to by Darwinian theory; his judgment has to fit the circumstances —and that is all.[32]

In my opinion, this characteristic of prudence has important uses in the evaluation of particular aspects of various cultures. Among other things, in the light of this rule we can understand better the mischievous influence of those political personalities (I hesitate to call them either statesmen or politicians, the one term being too noble, the other too pejorative) for whom political activity is the best of all amusements. Such a motive is in sharp contradiction to the nature of prudence, because it represents a desire to escape into extravagance in a domain which does not admit of extravagance. People with such tendencies would be better off painting surrealistic canvases; they also could play and amuse themselves with mathematical or logical constructs; or they could try to find new ways of making all sorts of things; but they should never have anything to do with politics. Unfortunately, a man who greatly enjoys action and power is hard to keep out of politics. I am not referring here primarily to the domineering type who really hates men but likes to manipulate them for

[32] See Yves Simon, "Introduction to the Study of Practical Wisdom," *The New Scholasticism*, 35, No. 1 (January 1960), 1–40.

the pleasure of being the boss. Rather, I have in mind people whom we may call political dilettantes. The harm done by them consists in trying to introduce extravagance into a system where it simply does not belong. And since this system is the public domain, whose state of excellence has much to do with the kind of life each one of us can expect to have in the community, the influence of such people can be far worse than just mischievous. But be that as it may, it is enough for us to recognize in the present context that, in contrast to modern logicians whose speculations remain scientific even if they are not logically useful, political dilettantes are engaged in activities which, while also not useful at all, are political only in appearance.

Finally, we come to the third intellectual habitus relevant to our theory of culture—namely, art or τέχνη. According to Aristotle's definition, art is the determination of things to be made involving the right course of reasoning. Can art be an activity of free development? The answer seems easy. The escape from objective necessity, the transcendence of objective necessity, occurs in art when the thing made is also a thing of beauty. What that thing is does not matter. In this respect, there is no difference between a temple, a bridge, a painting, or a symphony; even tools—that is, things strictly useful—can be made beautiful. We have recalled the romantic view that medieval craftsmen were at the same time genuine artists, because they produced things not only whole but also beautiful. There is a good deal of truth in that view: our museums are full of objects preserved from ancient cultures, which we now admire for their beauty exclusively, regardless of the use they once might have served. Clearly, then, in the determination of things to be made it is possible, on any level, to escape the objective necessity required by art considered as an intellectual habitus. But I believe that this aspect of art—

namely, the extent to which making things is no longer an activity of legal fulfillment but becomes rather an activity of free development—is most profitably discussed with reference to the fine arts, where questions of necessity and utility are not in our way.

MAN'S ART

We have had occasion repeatedly to compare work and the worker to fine art and the artist, and from this comparison we have established at the least the following two points. First, dependence on the pre-existent data, on what is given in nature and in the nature of things, is essential to work but not to art; that is why work is an activity of legal fulfillment, while fine art is an activity of free development. Secondly, considerations of social utility are essential to work but not to art; that is why no dishonest activity can ever be considered work, but a completely useless, even an immoral, thing may well be art.[33] What I propose to consider now is just how free man's fine art is and where, if there are any, the limits to its freedom are to be found. What I have to say on this subject should apply to all fine arts, but, in order to reach the decisive issue quickly, it seems best to take the case of a particular modern school of painting.

The term "surrealism" is said to have been coined by a poet friend of Marc Chagall's in reference to the latter's early paintings. Although, in view of the later developments of those who call themselves surrealists, whether Chagall should now be classified as a surrealist is debatable, for our purposes it is enough to recall that the term was originally applied to his paintings—and to the paintings of quite a few others of that period—because they failed, so to speak, to resemble

[33] See Yves Simon, "On Art and Morality," *The New Scholasticism*, 35, No. 3 (July 1961), 338–341.

reality.[34] It is also significant to note that at that time such art puzzled, irritated, and infuriated a considerable part of the public. Now, I believe that the deep meaning of surrealism is essentially related to the pride the artist takes in the independence of his work from natural appearances, even though this may be mixed with the pleasure derived from baffling people by painting women who have only one eye, or bodies that challenge the laws of gravity (as can be seen in the works of Chagall). The important point for us is that the label "surrealist" meant for a number of years precisely that the painter in question did not care to imitate reality. He was conscious of not being bound by reality, of being "above reality," and the question this approach to art raised and brought into focus was precisely whether "reality" was the proper concern for an artist.[35] That is also our question, but we must put it slightly differently and make it two questions. Thus we shall ask, first: Is it the nature of art to imitate reality or to be indifferent to it? And if the latter be the case, we shall ask, second: How independent can man's art be?

In order to answer these questions, it is absolutely necessary to deal first with the famous proposition that "art imitates nature," which can be found in many places, including the works of Aristotle, but which is not always rightly understood. That art imitates nature may mean either of two things. It may mean that nature produces trees and flowers, or men and women, and all the other things of nature, which the artist is then supposed to try to reproduce or represent faithfully once again through his art. For instance, here is a woman to be

[34] Cf. " 'Surrealism' is, in itself, a quite apt word. But the great contemporary painter who best deserves the name, Chagall (as, among the old masters, Hieronymous Bosch), belongs in no way to the Surrealist school" (Maritain, *Creative Intuition*, p. 82). See also Raïssa Maritain, *Chagall ou l'Orage enchanté* (Geneva–Paris: Éditions des Trois Collines, 1948).

[35] See André Breton, *Manifeste du Surréalisme* (Paris: Sagitaire, 1924) and *Qu'est-ce que le surréalisme?* (Paris: Henriquez, 1934). See also Maurice Nadeau, *Histoire du Surréalisme* (Paris: Édition du Seuil, 1945).

painted by an artist. Her hair is dark, so he puts dark spots in a certain place on the canvas; her face is shaped in a certain way, so he copies the shape, and so on. In the end, he has produced a resemblance of these data—i.e., colors and shapes —and he has a likeness of the woman. That is the popular, the unintelligent meaning of "art imitates nature." The other meaning is that the artist produces the work of art as nature produces trees and flowers, and that is what Aristotle means.[36] By "art imitates nature" Aristotle means art imitates creation, where "creation" stands not for the result of an action that has taken place in the past but for the very act of producing something original. That is the true meaning of "art imitates nature," which expression should not be used unless one has time to explain it.

It was Jean Cocteau, the poet, who once said "*La photographie a libéré le dessin.*" Suppose two hundred years ago a man wanted to immortalize his wife in the memory of his children, grandchildren, and great-grandchildren. What did he do? He hired a painter to reproduce on canvas a resemblance of this unique datum of nature, this given thing, this man's wife. But that is something that photography can do better than any artist, and so today the artist no longer has to bother about duplicating natural forms. He can do something else; indeed, he can afford to be a surrealist. An important effect of these developments has been that they have made it so much easier for all to see what has always been so —namely, that art as art does not demand conformity to pre-existent data. Why did successful businessmen ever hire artists to paint faithful portraits of their wives? Certainly not because that is the nature of art! The surrealists are clearly right in principle and so far as the nature of art is concerned. Art is independent creation. But what about the art of man, the art produced by the human artist? Cocteau has an opinion on

[36] *Physics* 2.1.

that subject too. But what does he really mean when he says *"Car la poésie, mon Dieu, c'est vous"*? To come up with a serious answer, we must consider nothing less than the origin and the condition of intellectual knowledge in man.

Plato is for all times the founder of the theory of intelligibility, for nobody has shown more convincingly that the distance between the intelligible and the sensible is qualitatively infinite. With respect to the question of how the apprehension of the intelligible takes place in man, however, I am not sure whether he believes exactly what he says; he may honestly be expressing his ignorance by referring to the existing beliefs. What we all know is that in the *Meno* and the *Phaedo* Plato propounds the theory of reminiscence—that is, the view that the human soul had a previous life in which it enjoyed communication with intelligible types or pure ideas. The soul was busy and happy contemplating these ideas, but then some sort of catastrophe took place, and ever since the human soul has been forcibly united to a corruptible body which inhibits the soul's striving toward truth. The problem of knowledge, therefore, consists in finding methods to get around the obstacle of the body and to reawaken recollections of the intelligible world of ideas. Again, this is Plato's theory of knowledge as expounded in these two dialogues, and I do not say that there are no contrasting tendencies in Plato. What is remarkable is that in historical Platonism the theory of the previous life has been taken seriously, both in pagan and in Christian Neoplatonism. In fact, this view has been popular off and on for a number of centuries, and I suspect that under a variety of disguises it might still be popular today.

The other major theory of knowledge is that of Aristotle. As far as the principle of intelligibility is concerned, Aristotle must be considered a strict disciple of Plato. For him, too, between the sensible and the intelligible there is an infinite qualitative distance. But at least in the mature part of the work of Aristotle, in the treatises that have survived, the story of a previous life of the soul and of reminiscence of innate ideas is rejected and replaced by the consideration that the union of the soul and the body is natural. To put it all in a nutshell, the reasoning behind and the consequences of Aristotle's position are as follows. Whoever conceives the union of the soul and the body as something forcible and unnatural is bound to hold that death is desirable. Yet the overwhelming fact is that we all dislike death, and even those who are almost ready to die are eager to live one more week, one more day, one more hour. That fact of life outweighs anything else, so that ultimately it is impossible to hold the union of the soul and the body to be unnatural. But if this union is natural, we are directed toward a theory of knowledge which explains the apprehension of the intelligible by some process of abstraction rather than by reminiscence. For if it is natural for the soul and the body to be united, then to have senses, to see, touch, smell, hear, and taste, and also to have imagination and memory—these are not hindrances to the activities of the intellect but its aids and instruments. In this theory of knowledge, our ideas are not produced by remembrance of past experiences of the soul but rather by abstraction from the experiences of the body.[37]

This Aristotelian theory, which is best outlined in contrast to the Platonic theory of reminiscence, is decisive for our subject. With its help we are led to understand that human art will never be allowed to be pure creation, because it never comes purely from within the soul. Human art is always the creation of a mind that from the beginning and inescapably is tied to data supplied by physical nature—that is, to things which art as such does not really need. Cocteau, the poet, was

[37] See Yves Simon, "An Essay on Sensation," in *The Philosophy of Knowledge*, edd. Roland Houde and Joseph Mullally (Philadelphia: Lippincott, 1960), pp. 55–95.

right: *"La photographie a libéré le dessin."* What this means is that the photographer has set the draftsman free by taking care of the duplication of natural data. Yet the freedom of the artist remains relative, because he is a human artist with a human intellect which operates by way of abstraction from sense-experience. Thus man's art can never be pure creation, and the other saying of Cocteau, the clown, becomes now also quite clear. He presents his proposition upside down, but we understand that it is convertible. *"Car la poésie, mon Dieu, c'est vous"* means also that God is poetry and that only divine art can be unqualified poetry, absolute poetry, pure creation.

Again, even human art as creation is free from pre-existent data. It does not have to imitate any appearances, it does not have to submit to any external reality, it does not have to reckon with any natural laws. If we are sometimes baffled and irritated by a surrealist painter, if we sometimes think that he should not allow himself such audacities, this is not because of the nature of art. It is rather because we know so well that human art *qua* human has its limits. A woman on a canvas does not indispensably need two eyes; she may have only one, even if she is depicted with full face. Picasso, in whose career is summed up all the metaphysics of art, is a great example. I personally prefer his great works of the earlier period, for though his figures do not coincide exactly, as in a photograph, with the outline of the models, there is more consideration for the natural data there than in what he has been doing in the last thirty years or so. It even seems to me that some of his later pieces reveal that he despises nature and despises the public also. He sees nature as it is very clearly, but then he distorts it deliberately, perhaps taking mischievous pleasure in asserting the creative power of that imperfect creator, the human artist. Socially this sort of thing is obviously effective. Picasso has remained a very popular artist, which tells us something about the present attitudes toward culture. Nevertheless, dissatisfaction with the way in which some contemporary painters have treated the data of nature, far from being evidence of Philistinism, may in fact evince sound taste. Painters should have some respect for the data of nature, if only because the human artist is not enough of an artist; and he is not artist enough ultimately because of the experimental origin of his cognition.

LEISURE, WORK, AND CULTURE

Finally, we come to the popular question of the relationship between leisure and culture, which is of course inseparable from the consideration of the place of work in human and social life. Let us recall the title of the book by Josef Pieper, *Leisure: The Basis of Culture.*[38] What does it mean? If it means that in order to do things cultural we need time to do them, it is fairly clear. For instance, studying classical literature is a component of culture of which many people are deprived who have to work from dawn to dusk, when they are completely exhausted and could not care less about the classics. But to say that we need leisure to do things does not seem very significant; if we call leisure the time left after biologically necessary functions and duties have been fulfilled, then we need leisure for work every bit as much as for culture. So, obviously, leisure does not mean just free time, but rather specifically freedom from work, as in the phrase "a life of leisure." Our question, then, must be put as follows: Is culture necessarily centered on a life free from work (taking the latter in the broadest possible sense as any activity of legal fulfillment that is also socially productive)?

The fact is that we can find several periods in history in which culture consisted principally of frivolity decorating the idleness of a distinct social class. The period spanning the late

[38] Note 2, above.

seventeenth and the early eighteenth century is a good example. In that period, even scientists, philosophers, physicists, and mathematicians had to be socialites and had to speak the kind of language that members of high society used in their conversations. To be sure, these society people were interested in both arts and sciences. But they considered themselves too refined to master technical scientific terms, and they simply assumed that anything really worth knowing or saying could be expressed elegantly in their own language. The works of Leibniz (1646–1716), for instance, are fairly representative of this approach and style, and this becomes quite evident when we compare his writings with, say, Kant's. Kant (1724–1804) no longer wrote for society people but rather for professional philosophers and serious students of philosophy.

Another example of this frivolous culture is the celebrated *Logic* of Port-Royal. This was a Jansenist institution used as a retreat by a few distinguished gentlemen of leisure (the most important of whom was Pascal), where, about 1660, two members of this group—their names are not important— fancied to write a treatise on logic.[39] This treatise is still being read, and there are some who hold that it is a typical example of Aristotelian as opposed to modern mathematical symbolic logic.[40] To me, it is just an historical curiosity. Indulging in an eclecticism of the second and third power and offering an aggregate of scholastic aberrations mixed with some Cartesian components, the book is altogether a logic-monster. But—this must be admitted—it is written in beautiful language. As I see it, what happened was something like this. When they came across logical subjects that could be expressed only in

[39] The most recent issue is Antoine Arnauld and Pierre Nicole, *La logique de Port-Royal*, edd. Bruno Baron von Freytag Löringhoff and Herbert E. Brekle (Stuttgart: Frommann, 1965). The latest English edition is *Art of Thinking: Port-Royal Logic*, trans. James and Patricia Dickoff (New York: Bobbs-Merrill, 1964).

[40] See Ferdinand Gonseth, *Qu'est-ce que la logique?* (Paris: Hermann, 1937).

technical terms, these *gens du monde, polis sur toutes les faces,* these would-be part-time logicians, seem to have concluded with really delightful naïveté, "Thank goodness that these things are of no importance." Yet some of the concepts that they dismiss so cavalierly are of the very essence of logic, and without them it would never be possible to say what logic is all about. But to the members of the Port-Royal group this did not matter, because they were not serious students of logic; they were gentlemen of leisure for whom culture was all decoration—all flowers. I sometimes wonder whether they would have cared had they realized that their culture was made of cut flowers that were soon to dry up.

In my view, the connection with a life of leisure which has often been held essential for the development of culture has to do mainly with what we have called above the flower-like component of culture. The structural component of culture, its hard core of intellectual habitus, does not seem to demand a life of social leisure, at least not necessarily. For instance, there is precious little leisure in the life of a philosopher who teaches fifteen hours a week at a university and must also teach in the summer school, because without that additional fee his salary would not be sufficient to maintain his family. The same can be said about a painter who is not yet famous enough to sell one canvas a year at some fantastic price, and who must therefore paint one picture after another to make ends meet. Even the scientist who is paid a handsome salary for doing nothing but disinterested, pure research in physics cannot be said to lead a life of leisure. True, none of these people belongs to the working class, but they are not members of a leisure class either. In the broad sense, they spend their lives working—that is, engaged in activities of legal fulfillment that are not only honest but also socially useful. But does that mean that they are incapable of contributing to the flower-like component of culture? Does it mean that because theirs is not a life of leisure they cannot break through, so to speak, into activities of free expansion corresponding to their habitus? I do not think so, as I have never believed that social leisure—that is, freedom from any kind of work—is an essential requirement of culture.

In our time there is much speculation about the possibility of a life of leisure for practically everybody, and the question of the relationship between leisure and culture assumes under these conditions a radically different aspect than it has had historically. In all the past experience of mankind, there was a division of functions between the many who worked hard to maintain society and the few who maintained culture and enjoyed a life of leisure. But as leisure comes to be enjoyed by the many, it becomes much easier to see that all that a life of leisure was ever able to support for any length of time were a few flower-like ornaments of culture. With more people enjoying more social leisure than it had ever been thought possible, we can now see much more clearly that, instead of a life of leisure, the real basis of culture—its supporting structure and hard core—is to be found rather in activities in the performance of which a workmanlike disposition is indispensable.

The immediate task before us, therefore, appears to be the development of a theory of culture centered not on leisure but on work in the broadest sense, including moral, social, and intellectual, as well as technical and manual work. Indeed, we may find in the most humble kinds of work those patterns and rules which can exercise a sound influence upon every search for culture and intellectual perfection. Let us say that technical work, especially on the level of execution, has the privilege of arousing in man a sense of honesty and an interest in perfection. Manual work is an activity which admits of no cheating. In intellectual work, particularly in its loftier forms, it is all too easy to cheat. For instance, take a theory designed to answer a philosophical problem. The answer is wrong, but the theory evidences a great deal of erudition and intellectual ingenuity; it is received as a magnificent piece of scholarship, and this brings the philosopher all the satisfaction he cares for. A manual laborer cannot expect satisfaction of this kind. The slightest defect in a key makes it impossible to unlock the door, and nobody can be fooled. Moreover, manual work is a field in which perfection is certainly obtainable. In many domains of intellectual work we are strongly tempted no longer to look for perfection because we know that we shall have to stop short of it. The temptation is very great for an artist, a writer, or a philosopher to give up interest in perfection, for they all know that their achievements are unlikely to be perfect.

But is such a thing possible? Can we really hope to develop today a culture that is neither frivolous nor obsessed with exploitation of physical nature? On the one hand, praising work and its prototype, manual work, seems to lead to the prevalence of the demiurgical ideal in our societies, sometimes called materialism. On the other hand, holding out an ideal of culture as this term has been understood in the last few centuries seems an ill-inspired remedy. If we cherish the element of refinement, of flexibility, of charm, and let everything which is sound—life, nature, energy, work, certainty, necessity—die out, we are confronted by the nihilistic monster which plagues, today, the oldest civilizations of the West and threatens to deliver them up to barbarism. Once they are cut off from the principles which make up the deep life of the soul, the blossoming externals of culture can only bring about a vacuum in which some kind of devastating frenzy is likely to develop.

Thus we must conclude that holding out an ideal of culture based on freedom from work is not the answer. Erecting such a culture into an ideal inevitably leads to a disorderly exaltation of the flowery element of culture, and this makes for subjectivism, arbitrariness, and an attitude of frivolous aversion to nature and its laws. Therefore, we must insist that knowledge of truth, not possession of culture, be our regulating ideal. And let us not doubt that, if truth is sought according to its own laws and to its own spirit, culture also will be attained. Everything is in perfect order if the factors of refinement, flexibility, and charm spring from what is strong and determinate and of itself hard. For lack of a logically satisfactory definition of culture, we may use a metaphorical one and say that true culture is a "bush of habitus" in blossom.

Years ago, in conclusion to a brief paper on the concept of work in a symposium entitled *The Works of the Mind*, I suggested that it was up to the manual worker to keep alive among us a certain spirit of honesty and perfection which ought to be carried from level to level up to that supreme sphere of intellectual life where all work comes to an end and the image of eternal life appears. The good worker and the lover of truth, I wrote, have much in common, and the promotion of their understanding could do a great deal for the reformation of our concept of culture.[41] Here, I wish to add a further suggestion. It is my feeling that our best immediate chances to begin to develop the culture with a contemplative ideal may lie in promoting collaboration between all kinds of technical work and the fine arts. Such a rapprochement has been enormously facilitated by the truly fantastic developments in modern technology, of which we should take utmost advantage. As a general rule, the more powerful the technique at his disposal, the greater the possibilities for creative choices open to any worker. I believe that once these creative possi-

[41] See Chapter 1 at note 6, above.

bilities are fully recognized, modern technology, traditionally held to be hostile to culture, could become an important contributing factor to the development of a truly humanistic culture.

Index

189